When You Read this Book You Will Know That

There
Is No
Trinity

I. D. CAMPBELL

Copyright © 2013 I.D. Campbell
All rights reserved.
ISBN: 1484920252
ISBN-13: 978-1484920251

TABLE OF CONTENTS

PART ONE 1

ACKNOWLEDGMENTS 1

MY INTENTIONS 1

PART TWO - A BRIEF HISTORY OF THE TRINITY 5
   THE BEGINNING OF THE COUNCILS 12
   ANALOGIES OF THE TRINITY 17
   THEORIES AND EXPLANATIONS 25
   GOD CAN DO ANYTHING 35
   JESUS (PBUH) THE BELOVED 36

PART III - THE BOOK OF REFERENCE 39
   ABOUT THE BIBLE 39
   BIBLICAL PROOF OF THE TRINITY? 45
   THE HOLY SPIRIT IS NOT GOD 48
   HISTORY OF GOD AS A MAN IN THE OLD TESTAMENT . 55
   WHAT WAS GOD'S PURPOSE FOR BECOMING A MAN? 57
   PLURALS 61

PART IV - REFUTATION THAT JESUS (PBUH) IS GOD 64
   JESUS (PBUH) THE SON OF GOD 64
   MESSIAH (PBUH) IS GOD? 79
   IN THE NAME OF JESUS (PBUH) 82
   SAVIOR IS GOD? 82
   LORD IS GOD? 84
   IMMANUEL 87
   THE MIGHTY GOD 90
   JESUS (PBUH) WORSHIPPED 93
   JESUS (PBUH) FORGAVE SINS 98
   LORD OF THE SABBATH 100
   MIRACLES 103

The Resurrection 110
Greater Than The Temple 113
The Seven I Am's 114
    I am the Light of the World..........................114
    I am the Door... 115
    I am the Good Shepherd............................. 115
    I am the True Vine 116
    I am the Bread of Life................................. 117
    I am the Way 118
I AM 120
Jesus' (PBUH) Preexistence 124
Alpha and Omega...126
Jesus (PBUH) the Creator 127
The Word of God 128
In the Beginning Was the Word 129
The Father and I Are One..................................135
Jews Wanted to Stone Him 139
My Lord and My God 141
Prophecies of Jesus (PBUH) 144
Jesus (PBUH) Taken to Heaven 145
When You See Me, You See the Father 148
Jesus (PBUH) Is God's Image........................ 149
Jesus (PBUH) the Manifestation of God?.............150

Part V - Proof That Jesus (PBUH) is Not God 154
    Jesus (PBUH) Has a God 154
    Jesus (PBUH) in His Glory and Essence 160
    Is Jesus (PBUH) Sinless? 161
    Did People Think That Jesus (PBUH) Was God? ..162
    Equal with God, and of No Reputation 166
    Scribe Asks Jesus (PBUH) a Critical Question ...170
    Some Forseeable Rebuttals to My Claims 173
    The Least Fantastic Explanation 175
    For the Average Christian 177
    The Father Is God 180

  Jesus (Pbuh) Servant of God, Not Son of God ...183
  Conclusion 184

Part VI - Al-Quran 189
  The Holy Spirit..189
  Jesus (Pbuh) the Servant of Allah 192
  The Trinity and God the Father 205
  The Truth Has Arrived..208

ABOUT THE AUTHOR

Mr. Campbell was raised attending both the Christian Church and the Muslim Mosque. He was always inquisitive about religion. Around the age of 14, he decided that Islam was the path for him. However, he was rather secretive about his belief due to the negative perception many had of the religion. When Islam became the topic of any discussion, he maintained the Islamic sympathizer role as the son of a Muslim, while being careful not to be identified as a Muslim himself. The stigma surrounding Islam and Muslims only intensified throughout the years, but so too did his desire to announce to the world that ISLAM IS THE TRUTH. Throughout his life, he had engage others in discussions on religion and a little over three years ago he realized that the issues that were raised in debate and in dialogue were issues which warranted extensive details, evidence and explanations. Drawing from all the books, lectures, and debates he come in contact with, and all the talks with Muslims, Christians, Jews, Hindus, atheists and agnostics, he set out to write one book which would convince all of the truth about the God of the universe. This one book blossomed into eight books which are written with the primary goal of proving the validity of Islam. It is with his sincerest effort that he wrote these books, with the hope that all readers will set aside their preconceived ideas and have an open mind.

BOOKS BY THIS AUTHOR INCLUDE:

"Islam Is The Truth"
"Jesus Was Not Crucified"
"The Jewish Torah Is Not The Word Of God"
"There Is No Trinity"
"25 Myths About Islam"
"GOD The Irresistible"
"FAQs About Islam"
"What God Says About Jesus"

FOR INFORMATION ON PURCHASING THESE BOOKS
VISIT:
WWW.ISLAMISTHETRUTH.ORG

This book is dedicated to Yahya Luqman Saleem

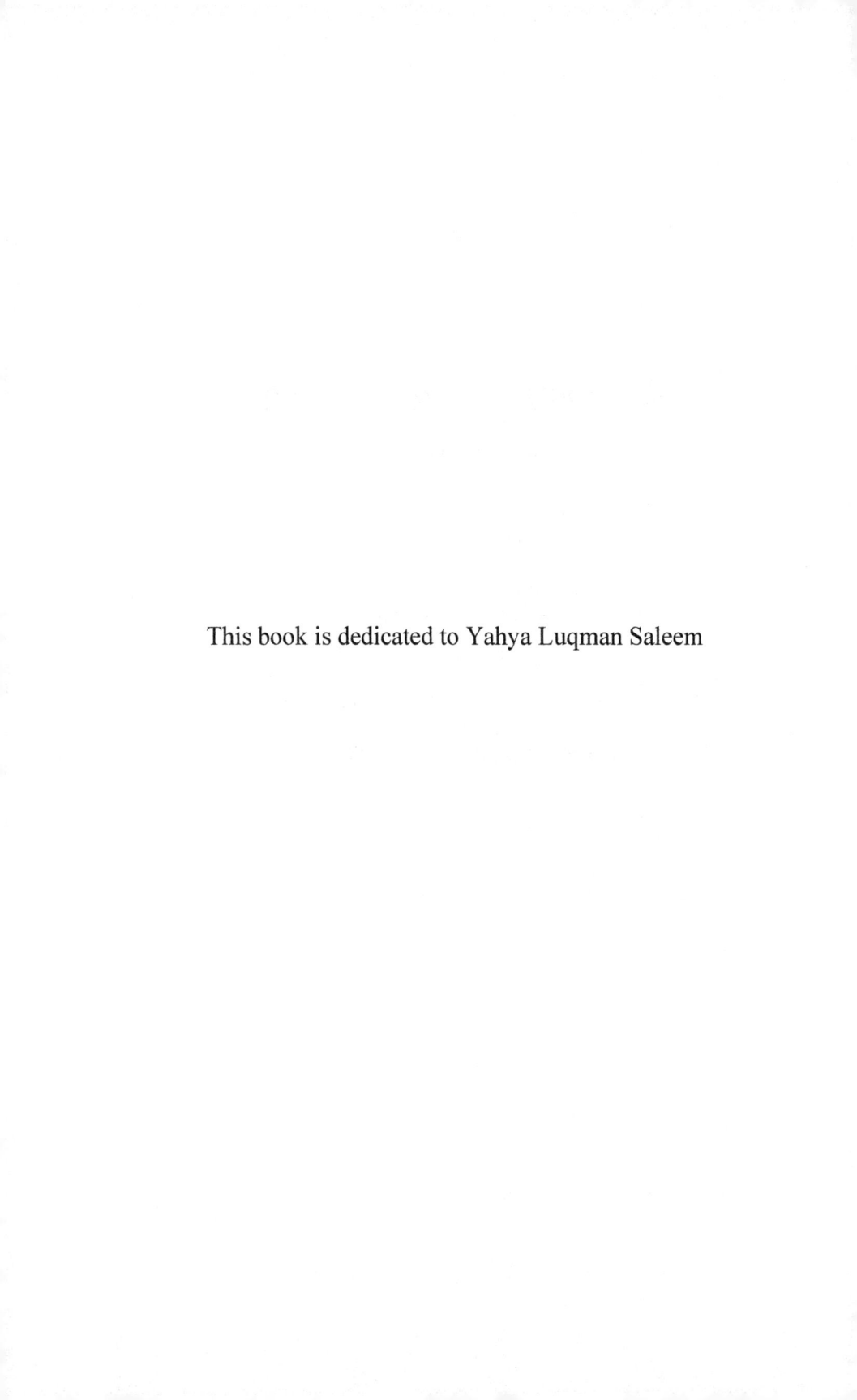

BISMILLAHI RAHMANI RAHEEM-IN THE NAME OF ALLAH MOST GRACIOUS, MOST MERCIFUL

If You Open Your Heart And You Open Your Mind, When You Read This Book It Will Open Your Eyes.

PART ONE

ACKNOWLEDGMENTS

First and foremost, ALHAMDULILAH. ALL PRAISE IS DUE TO ALLAH. He is the source of all truth, therefore all that I convey of the truth in this book and in life are because of ALLAH, and only the mistakes are from me.

MY INTENTIONS

"If Jesus is not God, then there is no Christianity, and we who worship Him are nothing more than idolaters. Conversely, if He is God, those who say he was merely a good man, or even the best of men, are blasphemers. More serious still, if He is not God, then He is a blasphemer in the fullest sense of the word. If He is not God, He is not even good....The very basis of Christianity is that Jesus was God manifest in the flesh (1Timothy 3:16). If that assertion can be overthrown, then the whole superstructure of Christianity crashes to the ground, and we are bound to assume that Jesus was either a shameless impostor or that He suffered from a delusion."
(The Incomparable Christ, J. Oswald Sanders p.53)

I chose this quote because it implicates me and my faith as well as those who are subscribers to the doctrine of the

Trinity. Since both parties run the risk of the egregious sin of blasphemy in the eyes of the God in which we serve, it is imperative that this topic is concisely examined. Yet this quote also places shackles on anyone declaring that Jesus is not God. One is given two options, either Jesus is God or he is a liar. Are there only two options? We shall see.

Al-Qur'an 4:171 *DON'T SAY TRINITY! Stop it! It will be better for you. For GOD is one GOD.*

This is the sentiment presented in the Muslim's holy book, the Qur'an. I would suggest that the message that it intends to convey is that the idea of Trinity, specifically the doctrine understood by those who profess to be followers of the Prophet Isa, as Christians call him in English, Jesus (pbuh), is not constant with the term "monotheism." I believe the Qur'an is proclaiming that the belief in the Trinity is actually not monotheism (the belief in one God), but polytheism (the belief in many Gods) or henotheism (devotion to one God, with acceptance of other gods). As I believe the Qur'an to be literally the "WORDS OF GOD," I intended to demonstrate the truth of the message contained in this verse of the Qur'an.

However, I would first like to demonstrate this point from the Bible and other Christian sources. Upon completion of this, I will present the Qur'anic view on the subject, which the title more than alludes to. It has been, at times, the prerogative of overzealous evangelist Christians to declare evidence for the Trinity to be contained in the Qur'an.

For this purpose, I want to show that the doctrine will not stand with its supposed primary source (the Bible) first, so it is of no consequence if the Trinity is actually supported by the Qur'an.

Unfortunately for the evangelist, the Qur'an is in total opposition to and void of any hint of support for the Trinity. Because the idea of the Trinity is primarily described through theory, creeds and analogies, not from the text of the Bible, I found it obligatory to discuss these theories, creeds and analogies as well as other claims of Jesus' (pbuh) divinity, which have been cited by Christians.

More importantly, I would like to assure the reader that my intention in this book is not at all to insult or cause outrage from believers in the Trinity. I am commanded by God to "invite (all) to the Way of thy Lord with wisdom and beautiful preaching; and argue with them in ways that are best and most gracious" (Al-Qur'an 16:125).

With that said, the concept of God is a very sensitive subject. It is to be discussed with this understanding at the front of one's mind. Because of the topic's sensitive nature it is inevitable that its discussion will garner some reaction. I apologize in advance to anyone who may be offended by my words. However I am obligated to present the truth as I see and believe it to be, and everyone else is obligated to present their view of the truth, as well. This is how we are to arrive at the ultimate truth, by discussion and reasoning with one another.

Isaiah 1:18 *Come now, and let us reason together.*

There are more than 2 billion Christians on earth today. It would be foolish of me to not anticipate some form of response to the contents of this book. With this in mind, I intend to address any possible rebuttals to my arguments in this book. To consider and reply to every possible rebuttal to an argument is a daunting task but I will do my best.

PART TWO

A BRIEF HISTORY OF THE TRINITY

It may surprise some people to find that Christianity is not the only religion to adopt the doctrine of the triune god. There were Egyptian triads of Isis, Osiris and Horus, along with Ramses II, Amon-Ra, and Mut. There was the Palmyra triad of the moon god, the lord of the heavens, and the sun god. The Babylonians had the triads of Shamash, Sin and Ishtar. The Hindus Trinity consists of Brahma, Vishnu, and Shiva. The Romans triad was Jupiter, Mars and Quirinus. And the German triad was Odin (popularized in the movie, "Thor"), Vili and Ve which was compatible with the brothers Zeus, Poseidon and Hades of Greek mythology.

It has been argued that because these deities and their roles are not identical to that of the Christian Trinity, there is no real comparison between them and their very mention with relation to the Christian Trinity is a blunder. It is true that these triads are not exact mirror images of the Christian Trinity. However, similitude is not exclusively drawn by mirror images. In fact, there would be little discussions on comparisons of any two items, if the criteria demanded perfect reflection. With the mention of these triads, I am suggesting that the Christian Trinity place them in the company of those who are described as polytheists and that because of some glaring similarities in these triads with the Christian Trinity, it is not a blunder nor is it farfetched to consider that the concept of the Trinity has been influenced by pagan beliefs. Not to mention that the Greeks and Romans, both deeply entrenched in paganism, were the caretakers and deliverers of the message of Christianity to the world. In fact, all of the Hebrew Scriptures, called the Septuagint, were translated into the Greek language and the New Testament was originally written in Greek, despite Jesus (pbuh) speaking Aramaic. Also the Roman Catholic Church has been the dominant denomination of Christians since its inception nearly two thousand years ago.

The Hindus proclaim Brahma, Shiva and Vishnu to be the Tri-murti (three forms) of the supreme god, Brahman. Also, Vishnu is the godhead who feels such compassion for mankind, that he incarnates himself as men and animals to restore mankind to righteousness. There are some Hindus who believe Jesus (pbuh) to be one of Vishnu's avatars or incarnations because of their closeness in compassion for mankind. Noteworthy also is the Hindus belief of Vishnu's impending earthly return. Another thing to ponder is that the sons of these triads are begotten by their fathers literally. Many of these "gods" had children with mortal women and begot "man/gods" or "demigods" like Hercules, Perseus and Dionysus. Some may not understand the implications and importance of such a claim, but this a topic to be discussed in detail later on in this book.

Christian scholars and laymen have been aware of these similarities for ages. Some, such as Justin Martyr, have suggested that the devil sent imposters before Jesus (pbuh) to fool people. Others offer that the similarities are due to the thousands of prophecies about the coming of Jesus (pbuh) and their misuse by those who heard them to magnify a real person that they admired or a god in which they believe in. Whatever the case, it can be stated that if the pagans borrow from the teachings of the Judeo-Christian scripture, there exists a sense of reciprocity, because it has been well-documented that Christianity has adopted many pagan rituals and beliefs.

The Christian holiday of Easter is deeply rooted in paganism. Easter gets its name from pagan goddess Eostre. The name "Eostre" derives from the Proto-Germanic "Austro." You may notice that this is quite similar to "Astarte." "Astarte" is the Greek name for the Mesopotamian Semitic goddess "Ishtar." Incidentally, "Ishtar" is pronounced "Easter" and all three, Eostre, Astarte and Ishtar, are goddess of fertility. This explains Easter rabbits and eggs, as they are symbols of fruitfulness. Of interest also is Ishtar's relationship with Tammuz, a Babylonian god identified with two Sumerian kings named Dumuzi the shepherd and Dumuzi the fisherman. Tammuz was also said to have been sent to the underworld and later returned, thus he is considered a "dying-rising god." If any of this sounds familiar, it is because in the Bible, Jesus (pbuh) is referred to as a shepherd (John 10:11-14) and he was a great fisherman (Luke 5:1-11, John 21:5-6). Christianity also suggests that he was killed, spent 3 days in Hell and then raised to life. It is noteworthy that in the Bible, God showed the Prophet Ezekiel the error of those who worship Tammuz instead of worshiping Him (Ezekiel 8:14)

Now let's consider Christmas. Though the account of Jesus' (pbuh) birth described in the Luke 2:8 seems to indicate the time to be in the warmer part of the year, Christians celebrate his birth on December 25. This time comes from the Roman winter festival called Saturnalia in honor of the mythical god Saturn, the god of agriculture. (And of course, Tammuz was the god of food and vegetation.) It was a time of drinking, large feasts and gift-giving, just as Christmas is today. It lasted from December 17 to December 23.

In winter, the Romans' harvest was in need of sun to grow, so the "god of agriculture" was in need of the "sun god." Saturnalia leads up to the winter solstice. This is the time when the sun appears at its lowest altitude to the earth. It is the shortest day and the longest night of the year. After the winter solstice, the sun appears to begin ascending again. The sun is then is called the New Light. The New Light and the New Year were celebrated on December 25th which was called the "*Dies Natalis* of *Sol Invictus*," the "Birthday of the Unconquerable Sun." These celebrations persisted after the Roman Empire became Christian and they clearly influenced the current celebrations of Christmas and New Years. Undeniably, December 25th was chosen as the "Birthday of the Unconquerable SON (of God)."

Santa Claus and his reindeer are obviously mythical. Their origins are from the Norse god, Odin, who led a "Wild Hunt" of horses through the sky. The Yule is also derived from this Norse God. Not to mention, the decoration of trees is specifically described as a pagan ritual in Jeremiah 10:2-5. Christians believe in aspects shared by paganism such as baptism, salvation, communion, heaven, hell, and the birth, life, death and resurrection of a god-man. All of these have some form of reference in the Bible. However the holidays aforementioned have absolutely no justification in the Bible. In fact, the adherence to these holidays is condemned in the Bible, yet they were part of pagan culture and now they are a huge part of the religion of Christianity. This is mentioned to demonstrate that a significant part of outside culture can be integrated into Christian belief without sufficient grounds. I believe the Trinity to be a part of outside culture integrated into Christianity.

Nonetheless, the idea of the Trinity and the divinity of Jesus (pbuh) have long been in dispute. Early Christian groups like the Ebionites, Cerinthians and several others denied the divinity of Jesus (The Cerinthians and the Basilians also deny Jesus' crucifixion). The first Christians were, of course, Jews who were nicknamed Christians, alluding to their following of Jesus Christ (pbuh). What is to be commented on is the fact that these early Christians were allowed to worship in the Jewish synagogues. "They keep up their daily attendance at the Temple" (Acts 2:46). This would be highly unlikely if we assume that these early Christians were worshiping God in a Trinity.

The book of Acts documents several instances of the early Christians in synagogues proclaiming Jesus (pbuh) to be the Messiah. However to extend the leniency of the Jews to allow the actual worship of a man (whom they had killed) along with two other entities is improbable in the synagogues and especially in the Holy Temple. This would be and is today an egregious and intolerable form of blasphemy to Jews, punishable by death (Deut. 13:6-10). Not to mention, the proposed view that Jesus (pbuh), in essence or in fact (depending on the church in which you belong), negated all the laws of Moses (pbuh). To ascribe such dogmas to early Christians may be in folly.

The admittance of early Christians to the synagogue and the Temple may be best explained by the Muslim's view that Jesus' (pbuh) brought no new doctrine, but the continuation of Moses' (pbuh) law and that he never attributed divinity to himself. These beliefs would have been much more acceptable to Jews than its counterpart. This line of thinking was echoed by University of Richmond professor, Dr. Robert Alley, who the Washington Post (January 5, 1978) reported lost his chairmanship of the Department of Religion.

"....The (Biblical) passages where Jesus talks about the Son of God are later additions.... what the church said about him. Such a claim of deity for himself would not have been consistent with his entire lifestyle as we can reconstruct. For the first three decades after Jesus' death, Christianity continued as a sect within Judaism. The first three decades of the existence of the church were within the synagogue. That would have been beyond belief if they (the followers) had boldly proclaimed the deity of Jesus."

To this day, the doctrine of the Trinity is eschewed by many churches throughout Asia, and Africa, as well as

Unitarian churches and the Jehovah's Witnesses. In the British newspaper the "Daily News" 25/6/84 an article entitled "Shock survey of Anglican Bishops" reports:

"More than half of England's Anglican Bishops say that Christians are not obliged to believe that Jesus Christ was God, according to a survey published today. The pole of 31 of England's 39 bishops shows that many of them think that Christ's miracles, the virgin birth and the resurrection might not have happened exactly as described in the Bible. Only 11 of the bishops insisted that Christians must regard Christ as both God and man, while 19 said it was sufficient to regard Jesus as "God's supreme agent."

The idea of the Trinity has evolved into what it is today, though many believe that it was taught by Jesus (pbuh), or at least his disciples. The Catholic Encyclopedia attests to the fact that the Trinity was finalized 3 centuries after Jesus (pbuh).

"........There is also the closely parallel recognition on the part of historians of dogma and systematic theologians that when one does speak of an unqualified Trinitarianism, one has moved from the period of Christian origins to, say, the last quadrant of the 4th century. It was only then that what might be called the definitive Trinitarian dogma 'One God in three Persons' became thoroughly assimilated into Christian life and thought ... it was the product of 3 centuries of doctrinal development."
"The New Catholic Encyclopedia," Volume XIV, p. 295

Quintus Septimius Florens Tertullianus (155-225), a church leader and Christian author, was the first to use the term "trinity" as he described the Christian understanding of the doctrine. It is Tertullianus who said "These three are one substance, not one person; and it is said, 'I and my Father are one' in respect not of the singularity of number but the unity of the substance." (Adv. Praxeam, ix.)

It is obvious that Tertullianus' declaration didn't settle the matter. The proliferation of Christianity in Rome, ruled and populated by pagans, was of great concern to its emperor Constantine. Even more disturbing was the intellectual war brewing over the Trinity and Jesus' (pbuh) divinity between Arius, a presbyter of Alexandria, and Alexander, the bishop of Alexandria. Alexander insisted that Jesus (pbuh) was the same substance (homoecious) as the Father. Arius considered this heresy. He was convinced that the Father was God only and Jesus (pbuh) was but a human being and a Prophet of God. These men and their followers argued excessively.

THE BEGINNING OF THE COUNCILS

2Timothy 4:3 *For the time will come when men will not put up with sound doctrine. Instead, to suit their own desires, they will gather around them a great number of teachers to say what their itching ears want to hear.*

In an effort to simmer down the tensions, Constantine assembled the 1st Council of Nicea to settle their dispute in 325 A.D. Interestingly enough, the date for Easter was established at this council, as well. The pagan Emperor presided over the council and it was a majority DECISION that Jesus (pbuh) was of the same substance as God the Father. As a consequent of this vote Alexander, Athanasius (the deacon of the Council of Nicea) and Constantine had Arius exiled to Illyria. Though proponents of the Trinity have held that Constantine played a rather minor role in guiding the final decisions at the council, those opposed to the Trinity have suggested otherwise. Encyclopedia Britannica and the American Academic Encyclopedia are two sources that support the idea that Constantine, a pagan until his deathbed conversion to Christianity, played a considerable part in the development of one of Christianity's most highly disputed doctrines.

According to the Encyclopedia Britannica: "Constantine himself presided, actively guiding the discussions and personally proposed the crucial formula expressing the relationship of Christ to God in the creed issued by the council, 'of one substance with the Father.'"

The American Academic Encyclopedia states: "Although this was not Constantine's first attempt to reconcile factions in Christianity, it was the first time he had used the imperial office to impose a settlement."

With religion's most sacred doctrine, the nature of God, being interpreted and facilitated by great Greek philosophers like Athanasius, Alexander, and Origen, overseen by the Roman Emperor Constantine and influenced by the likes of Greek philosopher Plato, it is little wonder as to why the Trinity is accused of having pagan origins. Greeks and Romans had gods beyond counting. It would be easy for them to believe in a Father, a Son and a Spirit who are one God. It is extremely possible and plausible that these Greeks took words and saying of the Bible that were metaphorical and interpreted them literally, reconciling their pagan beliefs with the newly found Christian doctrine.

II. A Brief History of the Trinity

After the Trinitarians victory in the 1st council, the churches assembled 13 more times in order to formulate the doctrine of the Trinity and its understanding into its present form. The Athanasian Creed, which was authored by Athanasius, was written at the 1st council of Nicea 325 A.D. It reads as follows:

1. Whosoever will be saved, before all things it is necessary that he hold the catholic faith;
2. Which faith except every one do keep whole and undefiled, without doubt he shall perish everlastingly.
3. And the catholic faith is this: That we worship one God in Trinity, and Trinity in Unity;
4. Neither confounding the persons nor dividing the substance.
5. For there is one person of the Father, another of the Son, and another of the Holy Spirit.
6. But the Godhead of the Father, of the Son, and of the Holy Spirit is all one, the glory equal, the majesty coeternal.
7. Such as the Father is, such is the Son, and such is the Holy Spirit.
8. The Father uncreate, the Son uncreate, and the Holy Spirit uncreate.
9. The Father incomprehensible, the Son incomprehensible, and the Holy Spirit incomprehensible.
10. The Father eternal, the Son eternal, and the Holy Spirit eternal.
11. And yet they are not three eternals but one eternal.
12. As also there are not three untreated nor three incomprehensible, but one untreated and one incomprehensible.
13. So likewise the Father is almighty, the Son almighty, and the Holy Spirit almighty.

14. And yet they are not three almighties, but one almighty.
15. So the Father is God, the Son is God, and the Holy Spirit is God;
16. And yet they are not three Gods, but one God.
17. So likewise the Father is Lord, the Son Lord, and the Holy Spirit Lord;
18. And yet they are not three Lords but one Lord.
19. For like as we are compelled by the Christian verity to acknowledge every Person by himself to be God and Lord;
20. So are we forbidden by the catholic religion to say; There are three Gods or three Lords.
21. The Father is made of none, neither created nor begotten.
22. The Son is of the Father alone; not made nor created, but begotten.
23. The Holy Spirit is of the Father and of the Son; neither made, nor created, nor begotten, but proceeding.
24. So there is one Father, not three Fathers; one Son, not three Sons; one Holy Spirit, not three Holy Spirits.
25. And in this Trinity none is afore or after another; none is greater or less than another.
26. But the whole three persons are coeternal, and coequal.
27. So that in all things, as aforesaid, the Unity in Trinity and the Trinity in Unity is to be worshiped.
28. He therefore that will be saved must thus think of the Trinity.
29. Furthermore, it is necessary to everlasting salvation that he also believe rightly the incarnation of our Lord Jesus Christ.
30. For the right faith is that we believe and confess that our Lord Jesus Christ, the Son of God, is God and man.
31. God of the substance of the Father, begotten before the worlds; and man of substance of His mother, born in the world.

32. Perfect God and perfect man, of a reasonable soul and human flesh subsisting.
33. Equal to the Father as touching His Godhead, and inferior to the Father as touching His manhood.
34. Who, although He is God and man, yet He is not two, but one Christ.
35. One, not by conversion of the Godhead into flesh, but by taking of that manhood into God.
36. One altogether, not by confusion of substance, but by unity of person.
37. For as the reasonable soul and flesh is one man, so God and man is one Christ;
38. Who suffered for our salvation, descended into hell, rose again the third day from the dead;
39. He ascended into heaven, He sits on the right hand of the Father, God, Almighty;
40. From thence He shall come to judge the quick and the dead.
41. At whose coming all men shall rise again with their bodies;
42. and shall give account of their own works.
43. And they that have done good shall go into life everlasting and they that have done evil into everlasting fire.
44. This is the catholic faith, which except a man believe faithfully he cannot be saved.

The Nicene Creed was also adopted at The 1st Council of Nicea and authored by Athanasius and it appears in the Council of Chalcedon A.D. 451 which seems to be a shorten version of the Athanasian Creed.

We believe in one God the Father Almighty, Maker of heaven and earth, and of all things visible and invisible.

And in one Lord Jesus Christ, the only-begotten Son of God, begotten of the Father before all worlds, God of God, Light of Light, Very God of Very God, begotten, not made, being of one substance with the Father by whom all things were made; who for us men, and for our salvation, came down from heaven, and was incarnate by the Holy Spirit of the Virgin Mary, and was made man, and was crucified also for us under Pontius Pilate. He suffered and was buried, and the third day he rose again according to the Scriptures, and ascended into heaven, and sitteth on the right hand of the Father. And he shall come again with glory to judge both the quick and the dead, whose kingdom shall have no end.

Added to the Nicene Creed at the Council of Constantinople 381 A.D. is the following:

We believe in the Holy Spirit, the Lord and Giver of Life, who proceedeth from the Father and the Son, who with the Father and the Son together is worshipped and glorified, who spoke by the prophets. And we believe one holy catholic and apostolic Church. We acknowledge one baptism for the remission of sins. And we look for the resurrection of the dead, and the life of the world to come. Amen.

More than 300 years had elapsed after Jesus' (pbuh) time on earth before the doctrine of Trinity was established. Despite the numerous biographies of Jesus (pbuh) and the writings about his life and mission, included and excluded from the Bible, the most important aspect of Christianity was unanswered for 300 years. Not one of these authors explicitly said that Jesus (pbuh) was God or that God was a triune god, so it was left to people's opinion, and interpretation.

ANALOGIES OF THE TRINITY

In the explanation of this doctrine of the Trinity, you will find endless analogies to help better understand this complex notion of three persons that equal one god. Triangles, three-leaf clovers, fruits, cats, and ants are all items used to describe the nature of the Almighty God of the Universe. For a system of belief not explicitly defined in the Bible, it becomes imperative for scholars to use some form of reference to help explain the Trinity.

Some are honest enough to admit that no comparison is sufficient enough to explain the Trinity. However, this doesn't deter the others from presenting countless new analogies, such as:

-The Father is the Sun; the Son is the Light, and the Holy Spirit is Heat
-Roots, trunk, and branches are parts of one tree.
-You are mind, body and soul but one person.
-An egg consists of yolk, the white and the shell.
-Water can be a solid, liquid or gas.
-A man can be a husband, a father and a son simultaneously.
-Time has three dimensions, past, present, and future.
-Space also has three dimensions, height, width and depth.
-A three-leaf clover has 3 different leaves but it is one flower.
-Fruit is composed of the seeds, core and shell, yet it is one piece of fruit.

Here are more real life examples.

Christians use the example of the Moon rock sample brought back from Neil Armstrong's trip to the Moon. They assert that the Moon rock is a part of the Moon and it can be used by man to understand the nature of the moon. God is the Moon in this analogy and Jesus(pbuh) is depicted as the Moon rock.

H. Mollegen offers: "The light (the Father) shines through the colored slide (the Son) to cast an image (the Holy Spirit) on the screen (the church)."

The Father, Son, and Holy Spirit correspond to what Sayers calls the Idea, Energy, and Power. For a writer, the Idea is the book as he first imagines it; the Energy is the book as actually written; the Power is the impression it makes in the mind of each reader. The Mind of the Maker (Paperback), by Dorothy L. Sayers

"Let's take 'present' and add to it human nature. Present, then, would have two natures: time and man. If 'present' were truly human then he would be able to communicate with us, tell us much, and we could see and touch him. But, because he is also 'time' by nature, he would be able to tell us both the past and the future as he manifested the 'time' nature within him. If 'present' then, communicated with the past and the future, it would not mean he was communicating with himself, but with the distinctions known as the past and the future." -By CHRISTIAN APOLOGETICS & RESEARCH MINISTRY http://www.carm.org/doctrine/trinitylook.htm

"As you stand by the shore of the sea, as far as your eyes can see and beyond is the mighty ocean. It is an entity of enormous power, sometimes as still and calm as a tropical pool, sometimes rising in fury to smash those who dare to intrude upon it. As you observe, a swell of water rises offshore. The wave gathers momentum as it approaches the beach. Although it remains a part of the sea it has a life of its own. Then, after crashing high upon the shore, it returns to the sea from which it came. As a wave it had its own identity, but never was it separate from the sea.

Just as Jesus came from the Father and returned to the Father, He had – and still has – an identity of His own. The wave was never separate from the sea, just as Jesus was never separate from the Father. Just as the wave exemplifies the personality of the sea, Jesus is the personality of God the Father. If you have seen a wave, then you must have seen the sea. If you have seen Jesus, you have also seen the Father. And as you stand beside the shore, you become aware of another part of the sea. The salt air which invigorates you is also an integral part of the sea. It, too, has a separate existence from the sea, but is very much one with it. It penetrates everywhere and everything within miles of the coastline. As you approach the beach it is the signal that the sea is not far away. In fact, it is the sea – reaching out to you through the air. This is exactly what the Holy Spirit does. Just as the salt air draws men to the sea, the Holy Spirit draws men to the Father through Jesus Christ. The Spirit, although having a separate existence, is not separate from the Godhead."
-Robert Faid, "A Scientific Approach to Biblical Mysteries"

Admittedly these analogies illustrate beautiful pictures in the minds of readers. The soothing effect these analogies have on those troubled by the difficulties of the Trinity is apparent. But the first glaring point to be made is the hypocrisy of using analogies to explain the Trinity. This is, in fact, their argument used to disregard the similitude of Christian and Mythological Trinities because Mythological Trinities are not understood in the precise manner of the Christian Trinity. You may be hard pressed to find someone willing to suggest that The Father, the Son and the Holy Spirit relationship is equal to that of the components of eggs, water, space, etc. That withstanding, I find all analogies deficient in explaining the Trinity mainly because none of them reconcile the decrees of the councils brought forth to clarify the Trinity and the actual words of Jesus (pbuh). In my opinion, this is an impossible job to accomplish in the first place because the decrees and the utterances of Jesus (pbuh) are irreconcilable, as I will attempt to prove later in this book.

It is my observation that modern scholars of Christianity make use of analogies and their own explanation without or with very little reference to the words of Jesus (pbuh). There may be verses cited from the Gospels but many times they simply cite the chapter and verse without the actual text or the text is cited without the context of the event in question. This is because Jesus' (pbuh) teachings are in direct contradiction to the Trinity.

Therefore, it is important for Christian scholars to implore analogies and others biblical authors, mainly Paul, to justify the Trinity. I will also add that Jesus' (pbuh) teachings are in direct contradiction to Paul's doctrine of Jesus' (pbuh) divinity. Those in opposition to the Trinity are firm in their stance that Trinity is a doctrine foreign to Jesus (pbuh) and definitely far from his teachings, but it was introduced after his lifetime. In the gospels, Jesus stresses his message, but Christianity today stresses his person. If this is true, then there is justification in the claim that Christianity is not the religion OF Jesus (pbuh) or even taught by Jesus (pbuh) but a religion ABOUT Jesus (pbuh) as men interpreted his life story.

Nonetheless, the analogies are presented as explanations of the Trinity. Christian scholars themselves discredit analogies like, "A man can be a husband, a father and a son simultaneously." In the Trinity, there are three distinct Persons in one being, yet there is only one God. The problem with "the son, husband, and father" analogy is that you have only one person, a man. He's one man playing three different roles. This isn't the Trinity. In the Trinity, there are three different personalities. This is why Christians stress that these personalities never disagree and that they love each other. It's an ancient heresy called modalism, which teaches that God simply exists in three different modes, manners or forms. That isn't the orthodox, historic teaching of the church. Many Christians are modalist today. Unbeknownst to them is that their beliefs actually oppose the formula sit forth in Council of Nicea which defined the Trinity.

Other analogies which are eradicated by the Trinity's creeds are the arguments entitled "three-leafed clover," "the components of fruit," "the sun, heat and light," "roots, trunks and branches," "mind, body and soul," "yolk, white and shell," "past, present and future," "height, width and depth," "the moon rock sample," "light, colored slide, and church," "idea, energy and power," and "ocean, swell of water and salt air." These arguments are completely disqualified and become nonsensical when the components of each example are substituted into the Athanasian Creed.

The root is the tree, the trunk is a tree and the branch is a tree. But it is one tree.

Or the sun is the sun, the heat is the sun, and the light is the sun, yet they are one sun.

These examples become impossible when they are put into context. The first example contains components of the whole tree. They can never be considered as the whole tree separately as the creed describes that "the Father is GOD, the Son is GOD and the Holy Spirit is GOD, but it's not three Gods but one God." The second example includes the totality in the analogy, just as the "ocean" analogy does. Therefore, we can say for certain that the Sun is the Sun, but the heat and light are functions from the Sun, but definitely not the Sun in its totality. The ocean is the ocean, but the swell of water and salt air, both come from the ocean, but they are not the ocean in its totality.

The Moon rock sample and the cat can be grouped together, as well. The moon rock is part of the moon, not the moon itself. Also, a cat's skeleton is considered feline, but it is not a cat. The line "Perfect God and perfect man" of the Athanasian Creed undermines these analogies. In order for these analogies to be correct, the rock from the moon must not only be a moon rock, but also the actual moon itself. And, of course, there is no skeleton of a cat that is an actual cat.

Perhaps the best analogies used are that of "H²O," "space," and "time," because they fit the decree "the Father is GOD, the Son is GOD and the Holy Spirit is GOD, but it's not three gods but one God." However there are problems that must be addressed. H²O as a solid, liquid and a gas has the same components but they have different properties and they unlike the Christian godhead aren't "co-eternals," meaning they do not coexist in their pure state from their inception until their end. If ice is melting and it produces water and a small amount of gas simultaneously, then the analogy contradicts the notion of "coequals" in its function. Actually, none of the states of H²O have the same function. One can't drink a glass of ice or cool a drink with vapors. "Time" and "space" share the same flaws. It can be said that the past is time, the present is time, and future is time in a certain sense and yet there is only one time. Width is space, height is space, and depth is space, but it is one space. But the flaw comes to light when one considers the following:

8. The Father uncreate, the Son uncreate, and the Holy Spirit uncreate.
9. The Father incomprehensible, the Son incomprehensible, and the Holy Spirit incomprehensible.
10. The Father eternal, the Son eternal, and the Holy Spirit eternal.
11. And yet they are not three eternals but one eternal.
12. As also there are not three untreated nor three incomprehensible, but one untreated and one incomprehensible.
13. So likewise the Father is almighty, the Son almighty, and the Holy Spirit almighty.
14. And yet they are not three almighties, but one almighty.

This would mean that each dimension of time and space must have the same function and ability. But we know that they each have different functions and are completely dependent on each other to even exist. Also, each dimension of time is not the totality of time but a portion of time. The same is true for space, whereas the Trinity says each part is the whole.

St. Augustine offered this description of the love shared in the Trinity as proof of the Trinity itself. His analogy is "the lover, the beloved and the love" (The Trinity, Books VIII.14; IX.2, and XV.10). So, the Father is the lover, Jesus (pbuh) is the beloved and the Holy Spirit is the love.

To suggest that this proclamation explains the Trinity is inconceivable. If this was an apt description of The Trinity, one could just as easily form a Trinity substituting the devil for Jesus (pbuh) entitled "the Hater, the Hated and the Hate." (This may surprise some people, but the God of the Bible does hate, as he hated Esau in the book of Malachi 1:3. If he hated Esau, it is not presumptuous to suggest that he hates the devil.)

Trinitarians may very well respond that since I have dismissed these analogies as erroneously comparable to the Trinity, paganism should be dismissed in like manner. However, my argument is that paganism influenced the doctrine of the Trinity, just as the doctrine of the Trinity influenced these false analogies. Also these analogies are brought forth to clarify the Trinity. Considering that the pagan beliefs preceded the Christian Trinity, it is quite possible that Christian sought to adopt, and then clarify the pagans Trinity.

Theories and Explanations

Hebrews 13:8 *Jesus Christ the same yesterday, and today, and forever.*
Hebrews 13:9 *Be not carried about with divers and strange doctrines.*

Although creeds and councils were assembled, the difficulty in comprehending the Trinity was and is today far from settled. In 451 AD, the Council of Chalcedon was assembled to debate the nature of Jesus Christ (pbuh). If Jesus (pbuh) was God, then he was a God and a man simultaneously, or he was simply God in all aspects. That is to say, either he possessed two natures or he was of one nature.

The belief that Jesus (pbuh) only had one nature is called Monophysitism. The Monophysites insisted that Jesus' (pbuh) sole nature was divine. Many Christians who are unfamiliar with the concept determined to be the most accurate in describing Jesus' (pbuh) nature, will place themselves in the category of Monophysitism. This is partly due to the way in which Jesus (pbuh) is presented to them in their church. Some churches give no distinction to Jesus (pbuh) and God in the slightest way.

Whatever the reason may be, it leads their believers into what was pronounced at the Council of Chalcedon as heresy. Monophysites are not fond of the title given to them. They prefer the term "non-Chalcedonian." The problem with the "non-Chalcedonians" argument is easily diagnosed. The records of Jesus (pbuh) in the Gospels exemplify Jesus' (pbuh) human nature. For instance, Jesus(pbuh) grew in knowledge (Luke 2:52), he was tempted by the devil (Matt 4:1, Mark 1:12, Luke 4:11), and most importantly, he died according to Christians belief.

The list of Jesus' (pbuh) human attributes and actions will be studied more extensively, but the examples above are ample evidence against the notion that Jesus (pbuh) only possessed divine nature, as God doesn't gain knowledge (1John 3:20), he can't be tempted (James 1:13) and he can't die. Therefore to conclude that Jesus (pbuh) was only divine, yet he succumbs to all these things, would immediately mean that he is not co-equal to the Holy Spirit and the Father.

In light of this argument, the council members and the majority of Christians today believe in Diophysitism, that is the two natures of Jesus (pbuh), divine and human. This idea is also called the hypostatic union. Jesus (pbuh) is fully human and fully divine and these natures are united in him.

The Chalcedonian Creed reads:

We, then, following the holy Fathers, all with one consent, teach men to confess one and the same Son, our Lord Jesus Christ, the same perfect in Godhead and also perfect in manhood; truly God and truly man, of a reasonable [rational] soul and body; consubstantial [co-essential] with the Father according to the Godhead, and consubstantial with us according to the Manhood; in all things like unto us, without sin; begotten before all ages of the Father according to the Godhead, and in these latter days, for us and for our salvation, born of the Virgin Mary, the Mother of God, according to the Manhood; one and the same Christ, Son, Lord, only begotten, to be acknowledged in two natures, inconfusedly, unchangeably, indivisibly, inseparably; the distinction of natures being by no means taken away by the union, but rather the property of each nature being preserved, and concurring in one Person and one Subsistence, not parted or divided into two persons, but one and the same Son, and only begotten, God the Word, the Lord Jesus Christ; as the prophets from the beginning [have declared] concerning Him, and the Lord Jesus Christ Himself has taught us, and the Creed of the holy Fathers has handed down to us.

As was the case with the previous councils and creeds, The Council of Chalcedon did not settle the matter. Monophysites and Diophysites continued bickering over the nature of Jesus (pbuh). This argument brewed for 229 more years. It must be understood that in the arguments from the Council of Nicea to the Council of Constantinople, each participant used the Bible for the basis of their argument. Though views like Monophysitism and Arianism were outvoted in these councils, every argument presented is still held to this very day by some churches. Nonetheless, the 3rd Council of Constantinople, 680 AD attempts to clarify Diophysitism even further.

It stated:
Christ had two natures with two activities: as God working miracles, rising from the dead and ascending into heaven; as Man, performing the ordinary acts of daily life. Each nature exercises its own free will. Christ's divine nature had a specific task to perform and so did His human nature. Each nature performed those tasks set forth without being confused, subjected to any change or working against each other. The two distinct natures and related to

them activities were mystically united in the one Divine Person of our Lord and Savior Jesus Christ.

Let's explore the complexity of Diophysitism. The concept of someone being totally man and totally God is impossible by definition. But to begin, we must eliminate a new method used by some Trinitarians to fool its readers about Diophysitism. This method is to redefine certain terms in the Athanasian and Nicea Creed while ignoring the complete context. The method has been used on a crucial portion of the early creeds. The scholar proclaims:

The Father IS divine, the Son IS divine and the Holy Spirit IS divine (and there is one God).

This is a magic trick! This phrase may be presented without the ending to commit the deceit without possible indictment of dishonesty. The person mentioning this will have the listener focused on the word "IS." They will insist that the "IS" is used in predication. For example:

The book "IS" green.

This doesn't mean that the book is a color, but that it possesses the properties of a color, green. Therefore the "is" in the phrase "The father is divine, the son is divine and the Holy Spirit is divine" really means that they share the attributes of God.

The trick may be apparent to some, but when I was first introduced to the phrase, I was stumped. I heard a Christian apologist say it in a debate. Because of the research I had done, I didn't waver in my beliefs about the Trinity, but I was amazed to hear an explanation that I couldn't easily dissect. Then a correspondent of mine recanted the phrase on the internet. In print the magic trick unravels before my eyes.

While fixated on the word "is," the listener is oblivious to the speaker's real agenda, which is to change the word "God" to "divine." This subtlety seems insignificant but in it is a cruel trick. Though "divine" is used to explain the nature of God, it can in no way be substituted for "God" in the creeds and still be considered the Trinity. This explanation would have you believe that Jesus (pbuh) possesses the properties of God, not that he actually was God, in order to explain away some difficulties. But the creed says Jesus (pbuh) "is truly God" and "is truly man."

This is clearly using "man" and "God" as an identity of Jesus (pbuh) not as a description of properties that he possesses. Without using the words "truly man", the words "truly God" would be presented by the speaker as "truly divine" and none would be the wiser. Another line which reveals this trick is the actual lines that they misuse.

15. So the Father is God, the Son is God, and the Holy Spirit is God;
16. And yet they are not three Gods, but one God."

These sentences are crystal clear that God is not used as a predicate, making it interchangeable with another adjective, but God is used as a noun. Line 16 starts with "And yet," indicating that the word "God" is used in the same sense as it was used in line 15. The false claim would read in totality:

"So the Father is divine, the Son is divine, and the Holy Spirit is divine, and yet they are not three divines, but one God."

This illustration makes it clear as to why they omit line 16. It exposes their magic trick. Even if the last words are changed to "but one Divine," the word "divine" in this phrase would be a noun not an adjective, meaning that the usage of "divine" in line 15 is a noun as well. Another quick note is that passages from the Athanasian Creed may be pulled out to demonstrate that indeed they use predication. All the passages using predication will be arranged together to have the reader or listener convinced that ALL the passages of the creed are simply describing the properties of the godheads. This is another trick, because you will notice that the passages omitted from the discussion will be those using nouns of identity for the godheads just as was the case in the passage which was altered. Therefore, the creed uses predication and identity, but one must not be fooled into believing there is only the presence of one of these items.

The explanation above is in direct response to a well-reputed Christian scholar of today and it is repeated by his admirers as if it is the Gospel truth. Thus this explanation may come in handy. Another quick tip is to show that God the Father is God in his totality. This nullifies their argument, as well. But back to Diophysitism.

As stated earlier, the idea of someone being "totally God" and "totally man" is a contradiction in terms. God is not an occupation or a mere title that can be taken off and given away. You can't be promoted to being God and you can't be demoted from being God. It is what you are, not who you are. By nature, God knows everything. In contrast, a man is incapable of knowing everything. If someone knows everything, then he isn't a man. If he doesn't know something, then he isn't God. By God's nature, he cannot die. However every human born has or will die. Therefore you can't be able to know everything and be incapable of knowing everything, at the same time. You can't be mortal and immortal simultaneously. Yet, Jesus (pbuh) is reported to have been ignorant of the actual day of the Judgment (Matt. 24:36) and Christians around the world proclaim that he died. He is said to have done things that only a man can do, but God cannot do. How does one account for this?

Even though some will insist that Jesus (pbuh) was totally man and totally God, they will also say that the two natures can be switched on and off, like a light despite "two natures, inconfusedly, unchangeably, indivisibly, inseparably; the distinction of natures being by no means taken away by the union." Of course, there is no scriptural evidence to support such a notion, yet it is affirmed nonetheless. This must be so, in order to maintain Jesus' (pbuh) divinity and to guard the integrity of the Bible. But as with every explanation for the Trinity, there is a problem here. Problems always occur because the explanation is only for the difficulty at hand and it contradicts the remainder of the Christian doctrine. Any Christian will agree with these sentiments:

If you honor the son, you honor the father.
If you serve the son, you serve the father.
If you obey the son, you obey the father.

These are all tasks, like if you disrespect my messenger, you disrespect me. These two beings do not have to be the same in order to complete these tasks. But will the Trinitarian take this understanding further? If you KILL the son, you kill the Father? They say, NO!!!!!!!!!!!!! But why not? Because the human side of Jesus (pbuh) died, according to Diophysitism, not the side equivalent to the Father. If you ask a Trinitarian, "Why must Jesus be God?," undoubtedly, they will say a man can't bare all of humanity's sins, only God can bare all these sins. Then ask them, "well, who died on the cross Jesus (pbuh) the man or Jesus (pbuh) the God?" They can't say God died, so they are left to say that the man died. That means a man bore the sins of the world, not God. It's heads I win, tails you lose.

Jesus (pbuh) is also said to be an example for man to follow. He is sinless, void of the curse of the Original Sin because of his divinity. How can God be an example for a human to follow? According to this theory, he is a god/man and by nature far less inclined to sin than any other human being, thus not a good candidate for a human example.

Not to be outdone, another theory is articulated to clear this problem. This theory is what I alluded to when mentioning the "ant." They say Jesus (pbuh) was God in heaven and he was controlling an earthly body which was subject to man's needs and limitations. The analogy is like a man controlling the mind of an ant. The man is capable of lifting a huge rock, but an ant cannot. Thus Jesus (pbuh) knows all things and is all powerful but the man he was controlling didn't know certain things and was susceptible to death, fear, etc. Again the theory addresses the difficult confronting it, yet a "man" still bears the sin of the world. But even more interesting is that the roles assigned to the man in the analogy and to Jesus (pbuh) are not accurate. Jesus (pbuh) says ALL power is given to him by the Father (Matt. 28:18) and he can do NOTHING on his own (John 5:19). This silences the argument because we find that the Bible says the Father is the man and Jesus (pbuh) is the ant.

As Dr. Gary Miller, a famous speaker, often said, an explanation is not proof. This rings true with the difficulty of defining the Trinity. The creeds used are explanations, but are they proof? Are they coherent? Consider that we are made to believe that 3 equals 1, "Trinity is Unity." This could be almost understandable with the phrase "there are three different persons but only one God," just as four quarters is but one dollar. But the explanations is stretched too far when someone insists that four dollars is one dollar. This is expressed with the understanding that all three figures of the Trinity are God, Lord, Uncreated, Almighty, and Incomprehensible, yet there is only one God, one Lord, one Uncreated, one Almighty and one Incomprehensible. Christians claim that the Trinity is described in mathematics as $1 \times 1 \times 1 = 1$. To prove that the Trinity is actually suggesting $1+1+1=1$, one should turn their attention to the shield of the Trinity.

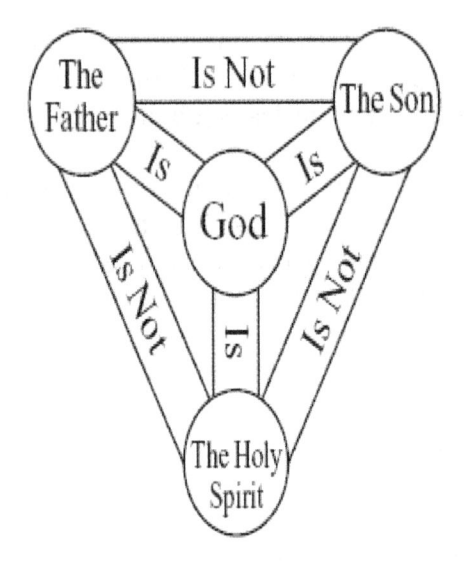

```
        The        Is Not
       Father               The Son
           Is          Is
              God
         Is Not    Is   Is Not
              The Holy
               Spirit
```

It shows that the Father is not the Son, the Son is not the Holy Spirit, and the Holy Spirit is neither of them. And they are God, and Lord individually, but collectively they are in one, this still means the sum of 3 equals 1. And the three are in unison about everything. This oneness will be dealt with later, but just to give an example of the refutation of this claim. One need not look any further than Jesus' (pbuh) last hours on earth, where he is pleading to be saved from crucifixion. He say to God, "take this cup away from me, but not as I will, but as you will" (Luke 22:42). So in at least once instance, Jesus (pbuh) and his Father were not in unison.

What about their existence? Are they truly co-eternal? According to the Athanasian Creed they are co-eternals, yet the Son is "begotten before the world was made by the Father" and the Holy Spirit "proceeded from the Father." From these words it is obvious that they are not co-eternals. Both Jesus (pbuh) and the Holy Spirit get their origin and he can do NOTHING on his own (John 5:19). This silences the argument because we find that the Bible says the Father is the man and Jesus (pbuh) is the ant.

As Dr. Gary Miller, a famous speaker, often said, an explanation is not proof. This rings true with the difficulty of defining the Trinity. The creeds used are explanations, but are they proof? Are they coherent? Consider that we are made to believe that 3 equals 1, "Trinity is Unity." This could be almost understandable with the phrase "there are three different persons but only one God," just as four quarters is but one dollar. But the explanations is stretched too far when someone insists that four dollars is one dollar. This is expressed with the understanding that all three figures of the Trinity are God, Lord, Uncreated, Almighty, and Incomprehensible, yet there is only one God, one Lord, one Uncreated, one Almighty and one Incomprehensible. Christians claim that the Trinity is described in mathematics as $1 \times 1 \times 1 = 1$. To prove that the Trinity is actually suggesting $1+1+1=1$, one should turn their attention to the shield of the Trinity.

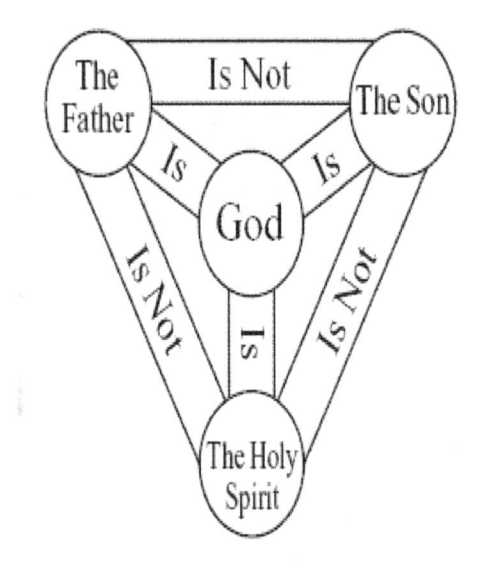

```
           The ─── Is Not ─── The Son
          Father ╲   Is  Is   ╱
               Is ╲   God   ╱ Is
               Not ╲   Is  ╱ Not
                    The Holy
                     Spirit
```

It shows that the Father is not the Son, the Son is not the Holy Spirit, and the Holy Spirit is neither of them. And they are God, and Lord individually, but collectively they are in one, this still means the sum of 3 equals 1. And the three are in unison about everything. This oneness will be dealt with later, but just to give an example of the refutation of this claim. One need not look any further than Jesus' (pbuh) last hours on earth, where he is pleading to be saved from crucifixion. He say to God, "take this cup away from me, but not as I will, but as you will" (Luke 22:42). So in at least once instance, Jesus (pbuh) and his Father were not in unison.

What about their existence? Are they truly co-eternal? According to the Athanasian Creed they are co-eternals, yet the Son is "begotten before the world was made by the Father" and the Holy Spirit "proceeded from the Father." From these words it is obvious that they are not co-eternals. Both Jesus (pbuh) and the Holy Spirit get their origin (though they are said to have no beginning) from the Father. The words "father" and "son" automatically means that one of them preceded the other. They can't both be eternal. The Father "begot" Jesus (pbuh). What does it mean to beget? Beget means to father, to sire, to produce or cause to exist. If someone causes you to exist, then at one time you did not exist and you are not eternal. To "proceed" from the Father is a little more ambiguous. "Proceed" means to go forward, continue, to issue forth or originate. It seems "originate" is the proper word to describe "proceed" as it is used in the creed. Therefore, the Holy Spirit "originated from the Father." It is the Father who causes the Holy Spirit to exist, thus the Holy Spirit does have a beginning.

Are the persons of the Trinity co-equals? Jesus (pbuh) says the Father is greater than I (John 14:28). This seems to contradict coequality. The argument has been made that this is the mortal Jesus (pbuh) speaking. The Father was greater than the mortal Jesus (pbuh). Perhaps, but what about the fact that Jesus (pbuh) says the Father is also greater than the Holy spirit, when he declares that the Father is greater than ALL (John 10:29). Yet the Athanasian Creed says "none is greater or less than another."

God Can Do Anything

If someone asks, how can one God be three when that is impossible? The response is "why are you limiting God?" "God can do anything?" Think for a moment. Can God really do anything? Can he lie? Can he cheat? No, he can't. If he lied or cheated, then he ceases to be God because this is against his nature. Yes, God has a nature. That nature is all good and all true. He can't be impure, evil or a liar. As Titus 1:2 states "God cannot lie." The idea that God can do anything is from a misunderstanding of the term, "all-powerful." There are those who conclude that the term means that God can do anything.

This is not the case, unless one is willing to concede that God could also sin. In that case, how are we to know that the scriptures in which we believe are not just a cruel joke from God? The Qur'an clarifies the idea that "God is All-powerful" by asserting that "God has Power Over all of his Creation." With a little probing, you will find that Trinitarians agree subconsciously with the notion that God cannot do certain things. If they insist that God can do anything, ask them "can God choose to be 5 Godheads, 12 Godheads or 27 Godheads?" They will say, "No, it is his nature to be 3." However the Bible insists that his nature is one.

JESUS (PBUH) THE BELOVED

Trinitarians say that the Father is a person, The Son is a person, and The Holy Spirit is a person. This is seized by their detractors as clear blasphemy, calling God a person. However, they mean to say personality. There is but one God, with three different personalities and personifications. This might have opponents of the Trinity allege that the God in which they speak suffers from the illness called schizophrenia. Just as a person suffering from this ailment may have more than one personality inside of him, so too does one God have three different personalities.

The Father is the strict law giver of the Old Testament. He is a jealous and wrathful God. Jesus (pbuh), on the other hand, is the loving and forgiving one. He has so much compassion for man that he endured great hardship to save them. The Holy Spirit is the one in the shadows with no true personalities. He is at the beckoning call of the Jesus (pbuh), if one believes him to be the Comforter (John 14:26). He can be described as the "Get Things Done" being in the Trinity. But Jesus (pbuh) says:

Matthew 6:24 *No man can serve two masters: for either he will hate the one, and love the other; or else he will hold to the one, and despise the other.*

If you are interacting with a Christians for any length of time, you will soon get the impression that Christians love Jesus (pbuh) more than they love the Father and perhaps they love the Holy Spirit more than the Father. The Father is seen as the being who gives men all these rules that he is bond to break, while the Holy Spirit aids Jesus (pbuh) in relinquishing man's culpability for breaking these rules. Go to any church or turn your television to any church service and within seconds you will hear praises for Jesus (pbuh). To a lesser degree, you will hear about the Great Holy Spirit. You may also hear the mentioning of God, but it is seldom the case to hear a sermon on the Father. This is because of their distinct personalities and job descriptions.

The fact that Christians show favoritism to one Godhead over another is one of the arguments used to combat polytheism. A person cannot serve two gods equally, as Jesus (pbuh) expressed (Matt. 6:24), even if they pledge sincerely to view them as inseparably. If you throw in another god, it becomes even more difficult to do. Take a look at Hinduism. Of the three deities in their Trinity, Vishnu, the compassionate God who incarnates to save mankind, is held in higher esteem than his counterparts. Even further, Krishna, one of Vishnu's incarnations is praised by many Hindus, more so than any other deity in the religion. This is the danger of having separate godheads. One of the gods is taken and shaped into what is most pleasing to the followers. Because he is more pleasing, they neglect the others. Those who read that their God is a jealous god should be very cautious not to fall victim to this inclination.

Romans 1:22 *"Professing themselves to be wise, they became fools,*
Romans 1:23 *And changed the glory of the uncorruptible God into an image made like to corruptible man, and to birds, and four-footed beasts, and creeping things.*
Romans 1:24 *Wherefore God also gave them up to uncleanness through the lusts of their own hearts, to dishonor their own bodies between themselves:*
Romans 1:25 *Who changed the truth of God into a lie, and worshipped and served the creature more than the Creator, who is blessed for ever. Amen."*

PART III
THE BOOK OF REFERENCE

ABOUT THE BIBLE

The authority by which Christians hold that Jesus (pbuh) is God is the Bible. The Bible literally means the Book or the Library of Books. It is a collection of 66 books for the Protestants and an additional seven books for the Catholic Bible written by multiple authors, many of which are unknown. Protestants reject the seven additional books of the Catholic Bible as unauthentic. They are referred to as the apocrypha, meaning "hidden things" or "doubtful."

There were at least 70 different gospels in circulation before the Council of Nicea. Athansius recognized only four of those gospels and 23 other books as authentic and his list is very similar to the New Testament of today. A great deal of the 23 books are the ideas of Paul written in Epistles, which is literally "letters" to groups of people. Many consider Paul to be the actual founder of Christianity. Oftentimes when debating Christianity, Paul's words are used instead of and sometimes in spite of Jesus' words. Yet, it could be argued that Paul never intended for his "letters" to be used as a great basis for all of Christianity, nor did he think that they would be used as scriptures from God. On one occasion, Paul confessed that God did not instruct him on a certain matter, but he will give his OPINION nonetheless (1Corinthians 7:25, 40). If his opinion is included in the words of God once, then opinions could have possibly crept in more than once.

It is noteworthy that the epistles of Paul were written between 50 and 60 A.D., the gospels (biographies) of Jesus (pbuh) were written between 60 and 100 A.D. So before the biographies of Jesus (pbuh) were written, Paul had already preached his interpretation of Jesus' (pbuh) teachings and established the Christian community. Paul, a confessed persecutor of early Christians (Gal. 1:13), says he saw a vision of Jesus (pbuh) and Jesus (pbuh) told him to stop fighting Christians and join them (Acts 22:6-11). It is obvious, from the amount of books Paul contributes to the New Testament that he not only joined the movement, but he took it over. Paul, after his vision, did not go and find the disciples who were with Jesus (pbuh) (Gal. 1:17).

Why didn't he? He often warned his followers of those preaching gospels contrary to his (Gal. 1:8-9). And he insists that he was not lying about his teachings (Rom. 9:1, 1Tim. 2:7, 2 Cor. 11:31, Gal. 1:20). One can only imagine what those other gospels contained and why he was considered by some to be a liar.

Putting the egg before the chicken, the books of Paul, which he calls HIS gospel (Romans 2:16, 16:25) must have been an influence to those given the responsibility of recording the life and actions of Jesus (pbuh). Even if the authors of the gospels were disciples of Jesus (pbuh) (Bible scholars say they were not), it would be impossible to accurately recount every word and deed that Jesus (pbuh) say and did considering the laps of time. But even the authorship of the gospels is in dispute. All four have anonymous authors, because none of them signed their name to these books. But tradition states that the authors are Matthew, Mark, Luke and John. Another interesting point is that Jesus (pbuh) spoke Aramaic, yet the gospels are written in Greek. As any translator of language will tell you, the meaning of words and phrases will always suffer, in differing degrees, with translation and transmission from one language to another. Thus the authors of these books have begun the task of recording Jesus' (pbuh) life with the inherent handicaps of translation and human transmission from human recollection.

The first three gospels, Matthew, Mark and Luke are called the synoptic gospels. The word synoptic is composed of the Greek word "syn" meaning together and "optic" meaning seeing. The synoptic gospels are those gospels which can be read together or side by side because they read in a similar manner and in a similar sequence. Yet the gospel of John has a style distinct from the other three, as well as narratives foreign to the other gospels. However there are some inconsistencies even amongst the synoptic gospels.

The idea of three different people, at least 60 years after Jesus (pbuh), writing the same stories, using the same style of language in certain instances, is not a coincidence. Bible scholars are convinced that the similitude of these gospels is due to plagiarism. "Who copied who?" is the only thing in dispute. The Augustinian hypothesis, The Griesbach hypothesis, The Farrer hypothesis, and The two-source hypothesis (this is the most widely accepted theory) are all theories which agree that the gospel writers copied each other, but the culprits are not the same. It is generally agreed that since Mark was the earliest Gospel, that it was copied by Luke and Matthew. Luke and Matthew also seemed to copy another scripture, which is usually referred to as the "mysterious Q." This idea is drawn from the fact that the two Gospels share a commonality in stories, sequence and details with Mark, but they also contain stories common to one another but these stories are not to be found in Mark. For example, the account of Jesus (pbuh) saying "he did not come for peace." It is in both Luke and Matthew, but not in Mark (Luke 12:49-53, Matt. 10:34-39). Other examples are that of Matthew 6:24 and Luke 16:13, Matthew 7:7–8 and Luke 11:9-10, and Matthew 3:7-10 and Luke 3:7-9.

Bible scholars conclude that they most have used another source to get their information because these stories are almost mirror images of each other in the original Greek. Since they have not found this source, they named it the "mysterious Q." Q is short for the German word, quelle meaning source, i.e. mysterious source. Luke testifies that there were plenty of people writing about the life of Jesus (pbuh), and he felt it his obligation to give a more orderly and accurate account (Luke 1:1-4). Perhaps he believed it would be more accurate to combine both Mark and the "Q."

The fact that the gospels were written 60 years after Jesus (pbuh), that the gospels are anonymous books, that it is widely held by Bible scholars that the synoptic gospels contain plagiarized material and that Paul had his brand of Christianity established before these biographies were written are irrefutable. The idea of the authors' opinions, beliefs, and preconceived notions possibly tainting their work is an issue by itself. Aside from the instance in which Paul admits having used his opinion, he blunders again in the book of Hebrews, which is "traditionally" attributed to him.

Hebrews 10:5 *For this reason, when he came into the world, he said: "Sacrifice and offering you did not desire, but a body you prepared for me."*

Paul is so convinced that Jesus (pbuh) died as a sacrifice for humanity's sins, that he misquotes the book of Psalms as a messianic prophesies.

Psalm 40:6 *"Sacrifice and present Thou hast not desired, Ears Thou hast prepared for me."*

Obviously preparing an ear and a body are two different things. Perhaps taking a cue from Paul, Matthew fills his gospel with acts attributed to Jesus (pbuh) to fulfill prophecies of the Old Testament, which are complete innovations on Matthew's part. For example, Matthew 2:15 states that Mary, Joseph and Jesus' (pbuh) departure from Egypt were a fulfillment of a prophecy by "the prophet." This is in reference to Hosea 11:1 which is talking about the people of Israel, who are called God's son. If we are to believe that this prophecy is in reference to Jesus (pbuh), we must also concede that Jesus (pbuh) sacrificed to the false god, Baal.

Hosea 11:1 *When Israel was a child I loved him, out of Egypt I called my son.*
Hosea 11:2 *The more I called them, the farther they went from me, Sacrificing to the Baals and burning incense to idols.*

Also each gospel writer seems to be of the understanding that Jesus (pbuh) will return and signal the end of the world before the generation he was speaking to passed away

(Matt 26:64, Mark 13:30, Luke 21:32, John 21:22). Unless we are to believe that the Holy Spirit inspires errors or that Jesus (pbuh) was mistaken or worse, it must be concluded that these authors wrote what they believed to be the case, not what was actually said and done by Jesus (pbuh). And there is more evidence of human error in the Bible. Again the culprit, Matthew blunders in the understanding of the Hebrews scriptures.

Zechariah 9:9 *"...behold, thy King cometh unto thee... lowly, and riding upon an ass, and upon a colt the foal of an ass."*

Matthews mistakenly takes this passage to mean that there are two animals, an ass and a colt, which Jesus (pbuh) will ride simultaneously. This is seen in Matthew's usage of the phrase.

Matthew 21:7 *"They brought the ass and the colt and laid their cloaks over them, and he sat upon them."*

The authors of Mark, Luke, and John avoid this mistake and state that Jesus (pbuh) rode the colt, which is the foal of an ass (Mark 11:7, Luke 19:35 and John 12:14-15). In Titus we find another error of the Bible.

Titus 1:12 *One of themselves, [even] a prophet of their own, said, The Cretians [are] always liars, evil beasts, slow bellies.*
Titus 1:13 *This witness is true.*

These passages contain what is called the Epimenides' Paradox. Paul, in this instance, quotes Epimenides' and commits a logical fallacy, by maintaining that the statement is true. The person who stated that Cretians are always liars is a Cretian. Therefore, if his statement is true, then his statement is also false. This violates the law of non-contradiction, because a statement can't be true and false at the same time.

These are but a few errors of the New Testament used to indicate that the primary basis for the Trinity and Jesus' (pbuh) teachings in general are built on shaky ground. Everything that is in the Bible is not completely accurate. There are mistakes, biases, misunderstandings, and opinions in this book. The good news is that despite these hurdles, the truth about Jesus' (pbuh) divinity and his teachings are still present in the Bible. One most begin to sift through to obtain the truth.

BIBLICAL PROOF OF THE TRINITY?

Every council and their creeds took great pains in explaining the Trinity. Many Christians assert that the hardships felt in defining the Trinity exists because it is a mystery beyond human understanding. This may be true, but the reason may also be that the Trinity is never explained explicitly in the Bible by Jesus (pbuh), his disciples or any author. The terminology used to explain the Trinity begs for Biblical confirmation and clarification. But what may surprise many is the fact that the word "Trinity" is nowhere to be found in the Old or New Testament. And though many use the words of Jesus (pbuh) to proclaim his divinity, there is no passage by Jesus (pbuh) unequivocally declaring his divinity. And for that matter, there isn't one iota of evidence that Jesus (pbuh) knew anything about the idea that the Father is a person, the Son is a person, and the Holy Spirit is a person and they form one God. In the 73 books of the Catholic Bible and 66 books of the Protestant Bible, there is no mention of this fantastic doctrine or any of the terminology used to establish its existence.

Though there are verses which mention all three persons, they don't articulate their divinity or unity. For example:

Matthew 28:19 *"Go therefore and make disciples of all the nations, baptizing them in the name of the Father and the Son and the Holy Spirit."*

Compare this with

1Timothy 5:21 *"I charge thee before God, and the Lord Jesus Christ, and the elect angels."*

Does this make angels part of the Trinity? The only passage closely resembling the doctrine of the Trinity is:

1John 5:7 *"There are three that bear witness in heaven, the Father, the Son and the Holy Spirit and these three are one* **1John 5:8** *and there are three that bear witness in earth."*

Yet this passage has been declared by Christian scholars to be an invention added to the Book of 1John.

"The text reads "the Spirit, and the water," and c., omitting all the words from "in heaven" to "in earth" inclusive. The words are not found in any (Greek Manuscript) before the sixteenth century. They were first seen in the margin of some Latin copies. Thence they have crept into the text."
-Bullinger's Companion Bible (footnotes) on [1John 5:7]

"Verse seven is not in the oldest and best manuscripts and should be omitted."
>   -Unger's Bible Hand Book [1John 5:7]

"This verse in the KJV is to be rejected...It appears in no ancient Greek MS nor is it cited by any Greek father; of all the versions only the Latin contained it, and even this is in none of the most ancient sources."
>   -Interpreter's Bible [1John 5:7]

"The text of this verse should read. 'Because there are three that bear record.' The remainder of the verse is spurious. Not a single manuscript contains the Trinitarian addition before the 14th century, and the verse is never quoted in the controversies over the trinity in the first 450 years of the church era."
>   -The Wycliffe Bible Commentary [1John 5:7]

In Isaac Newton's book entitled "An Historical Account of Two Notable Corruptions of Scripture" published in 1754, 27 years after Newton's death, he thoroughly explained that this verse was an interpolation (It had been alleged by many scholars that Newton was an anti-Trinitarian and he did not publish his findings fearing repercussions for speaking against the Trinity).

So it has been long documented that this verse is not to be found in any of the early Greek manuscripts before the 14th Century. This would explain the verse's absence in the numerous debates over the Trinity in the famous councils. It is very unlikely that no one for over 300 years would have mentioned this verse. And the presence of this spurious verse in the Bible doesn't help the Trinitarians case in the least. "How was it added to the Bible?"

More importantly, "why was it added?" To authenticate the Trinity, perhaps? What is even more peculiar is, though most translations eradicate this verse, the most popular version of the Bible, the King James Version to this day continues to be published and distributed containing this verse, despite overwhelming evidence that it is an interpolation. It is clear that mere interpolations are no deterrents for those obliged to continue the apotheosis of Jesus Christ (pbuh). Yet evidence of this deification is quite insufficient and the support to the contrary is in abundance.

THE HOLY SPIRIT IS NOT GOD

The Holy Spirit is believed to be the third person of the Trinity. It is referred to by numerous titles, such as the Spirit, the Spirit of God, the Finger of God and the Light of God. There has been a long dispute over the identity of the Holy Spirit. Many consider the Holy Spirit to be the power or force of God, while others insist that it is an entity in itself and it is distinctive from the Father and Jesus (pbuh). These Christians maintain that the Holy Spirit is not simply a force, but a person due to the fact that he is described as speaking (Acts 13:2), grieving (Eph. 4:30), and having a will (1Cor. 12:11). It should be pointed out that in the Bible, a donkey spoke to Balaam (Numbers 22:28) and it is not considered to be a person or to be God. Also, the notion of sin is personified as dwelling in man (Romans 7:17) as the Holy Spirit is in man (1Cor. 3:16).

In an even more illustrious example, sin is described as an old man's body which is to be crucified or destroyed (Rom

6:6). This is just to point out that things that are concepts and actions are giving life, personality and even a physical form in the Bible. It may be more accurate to take the Spirit of God to be a force or power of God. This understanding is to be found in several Roman Catholic writings, for instance, the New Catholic Encyclopedia, 2nd edition, article: Spirit of God:

"The OT Old Testament clearly does not envisage God's spirit as a person, neither in the strictly philosophical sense, nor in the Semitic sense. God's spirit is simply God's Power. If it is sometimes represented as being distinct from God, it is because the breath of Yahweh acts exteriorly (Isa. 48:16; 63:11; 32:15).......Very rarely do the Old Testament writers attribute to God's spirit emotions or intellectual activity (Isa. 63:10; Wis.1:37).

When such expressions are used, they are mere figures of speech that are explained by the fact that the RUAH was regarded also as the seat of intellectual acts and feeling (Gen. 41:8). Neither is there found in the OT or in rabbinical literature the notion that God's spirit is an intermediary being between God and the world. This activity is proper to the angels, although to them is ascribed some of the activity that elsewhere is ascribed to the spirit of God"

The idea that angels are attributed with some of the activities of the spirit of God would help better explain the presence of "Evil Spirits of God" in the Bible. Unless we are willing to concede that the Holy Spirit is, at times, evil, we must consider the option that there are numerous spirits of God, some holy and others evil.

The Christian view of fallen angels is angels which fall from grace and deviate from the righteous path. And angels are universally accepted as spirits, thus a good angel may be called a Holy Spirit of God and a bad angel would be called an evil spirit of God (1 Sam.16:14-16,23, 1Sam.18:10, 1Sam.19:9, 1Ki.22:22,23, 2Chr.18:21,22). And there is a mention of seven spirits of God in Revelations 5:6. This gives more weight to the idea that the Holy Spirit may be an angel, because the godhead is comprised of one Holy Spirit not seven. It seems the understanding that the Holy Spirit is God, might need to be reconsidered.

The Holy Spirit is described as a gift (Acts 10:45; 1 Timothy 4:14), which we can drink of (John 7:37-39), partake of (Hebrews 6:4) or pour out (Acts 2:17, 33). The Holy Spirit can be quenched (1Thessalonians 5:19) or it can fill us up (Acts 2:4). We are baptized with it (Matthew 3:11), thus it is stirred up within us (2Timothy 1:6) to renew us (Titus 3:5). These metaphors could help build a case that the Holy Spirit is a beverage. It is obvious that these metaphors are in great similitude to the metaphors used by Jesus (pbuh). Jesus (pbuh) said the bread is his body and the wine is his blood and his disciples must partake in his flesh. John 6:43-58 clarifies what Jesus (pbuh) is saying with this metaphor. Jesus (pbuh) is giving them the bread of knowledge and the guidance to God and eternal life. This same premise is spoken of by Jesus (pbuh) to the devil, when he says that one can't live by bread alone, but by every word proceeding from God (Luke 4:4).

Therefore, like Jesus (pbuh), the Holy Spirit is conveying the message of God and that is what we partake of, drink of and that which fills and renews us. [In the context of the

Eucharist, some Protestants have ridiculed Catholics for understanding Jesus' (pbuh) words literally. The Catholics eat the bread and drink wine and suggest that it is literally Jesus' (pbuh) body and blood. These Protestants find this understanding to be unreasonable and illogical, because it is obvious to all observers that it is not Jesus' (pbuh) body but bread and wine. But Protestants are victims of the same misunderstanding. They read about Jesus (pbuh) and they see that he is a man in all respects and most still formulate in their minds the belief that Jesus (pbuh) is God.]

Luke 11:13 *If you then, who are wicked, know how to give good gifts to your children, how much more will the Father in heaven give the Holy Spirit to those who ask him?"*

The Father gives people the Holy Spirit, just as it is said that God "gave his son" (John 3:16). This seems to imply that the Father has power over both the Son and the Spirit. And maybe we should ponder the idea of two parts of God being given as a gift by the Father. Jesus (pbuh) is said to have utilized the Holy Spirit. He cast out demons with the aid of the Holy Spirit(Matt.12:28, Luke 11:20). This may confuse some into assuming that the Spirit of God is superior to Jesus (pbuh). But if we are to believe that the Holy Spirit is the Comforter, then Christians must admit that the Holy Spirit is a subordinate of Jesus (pbuh).

The Spirit's arrival and annunciation of "all truth" are on the condition that Jesus (pbuh) leaves and Jesus (pbuh) sends him (John 16:7), just as the Father sent Jesus (John 20:21). To have our minds changed again, Jesus (pbuh) declares that blasphemy against the Holy Spirit will never ever be forgiven, yet blasphemy against him is pardonable (Matt.12:31).

One may be at odds as to who is in charge of whom as it pertains to Jesus (pbuh) and the Holy Spirit, but there is no doubt that the Father is supreme. Jesus (pbuh) says no one knows the time of the Last Day, not man or angels, ONLY THE FATHER (Mark 13:32). We can conclude from this statement that if the Holy Spirit is a person or a being, he is not all-knowing as God is.

Even more of a detriment to the divinity of the Holy Spirit is the utterance of Jesus (pbuh) in John 10:29, which says that the Father is greater than ALL. This negates the idea of the coequality of the Father and the Holy Spirit. Also the Father and the Son are often spoken of with little regard to the Holy Spirit.

The book of Acts gives us a picture of the Father and Son in heaven together, yet the Holy Spirit is described as a force used to help see the picture.

Acts 7:55 *But he, being full of the Holy Spirit, gazed into heaven and saw the glory of God, and Jesus standing at the right hand of God,*
Acts 7:56 *and said, "Look! I see the heavens opened and the Son of Man standing at the right hand of God!"*

The baptism of Jesus (pbuh) is another story of the three entities together.

Matthew 13:16 *And when Jesus was baptized, immediately he went up from the water, and behold, the heavens were opened to him, and he saw the Spirit of God descending like a dove and coming to rest on him;*

Matthew 13:17 *and behold, a voice from heaven said, "This is my beloved Son, with whom I am well pleased."*

This scene draws a splendid image. Upon reading this, one can't help but to envision Jesus (pbuh) coming from the water, a dove in the sky and a powerful voice coming from the clouds. Now, this picture in your mind, is it of three gods or one? At that very moment, where was God, in heaven or on earth? Strangely, the voice makes no mention of the Holy Spirit. Another thing to consider is the fact that this passage does not say that the Holy Spirit was a dove, but that it descending like a dove. Therefore, more clearly stated, the Holy Spirit at that moment came to rest on Jesus. He was not with Jesus (pbuh) before the baptism. Yet the Holy Spirit is said to have been with Jesus in their mother's womb (Luke 1:35). The Holy Spirit is said to have aided the disciples in their ministry (Matt 10:20), before Jesus (pbuh) left he gave them the Spirit (John 20:22) and Jesus (pbuh) says he will send him to them, when he leaves this earth (John 16:7).

It is obvious that the understanding of the Holy Spirit is a complex one, which it seems the authors of the gospels do not understand. Unless the Holy Spirit continuously deserts Jesus (pbuh) and his disciples or there are numerous holy spirits, these references are nonsensical. Even more peculiar is that Matthew 1:18 says that Jesus (pbuh) is "the child of the Holy Spirit."

So is the Father Jesus' (pbuh) father or is the Holy Spirit his father?

Luke 1:35 *And the angel answered and said unto her, The Holy Ghost shall come upon thee, and the power of the*

Highest shall overshadow thee: therefore also that holy thing which shall be born of thee shall be called the Son of God.

Unlike other passages which imply that the Holy Spirit is the force of God, this passage above shows that the Holy Spirit administers the power of God. This understanding leans towards the argument that the Holy Spirit is an angel. The angel Gabriel's name means strength of God. He is God's agent which displays the strength of God through his actions. In like manner, the Holy Spirit displays God's force and power though his actions. This seems to be the only plausible understanding that could reconcile his personification and his abstractness as well as his appearances and disappearances at the request of Jesus (pbuh) or the Father. If the Holy Spirit is understood as an angel of God, it may clear up many things which are to some readers difficult and confusing.

One last point to be made is that Mark 15:37 says that "he (Jesus) gave up the ghost" or "he gave up his spirit." Luke 23:46 says the same thing. The Greek word used for ghost or spirit is "pneuma" which is the exact same word used in the New Testament to refer to the Holy Spirit. This begs the question, was Jesus' (pbuh) spirit holy? If so, he was also a Holy Spirit.

If God is to be worshiped in truth and in spirit (John 4:24), is his spirit holy? If so, he is also the Holy Spirit. So there are three Holy Spirits? This understanding of spirit is not an idea that I just came up with. It is in fact Biblical.

1John 4:1 *Beloved, believe not every spirit, but try the spirits whether they are of God: because many false prophets are gone into the world.*

In this passage, we see that a true prophet is a true spirit and a false prophet is a false spirit. Holy is a description of the spirit and every human being has a spirit. So a wicked person would have an unholy spirit. Thus the devil, demons and Adolph Hitler are all unholy spirits, but they are not one being. All three have an effort in causing crime and sin to prevail over righteousness but they are not equal. The way we view these three evil beings is the way we should view the personalities composing the Christian Trinity. God is the supreme Holy Spirit. He gives the angels or the holy spirits the duty to convey God's message to mankind through a person deemed to be a righteous and holy spirit.

THE HISTORY OF GOD AS A MAN IN THE OLD TESTAMENT

The idea of God becoming a man is most likely derived from the stories of the Old Testament. God is described as a spiritual being in which no person can visualize without being consumed by death (John 4:24, 1Tim. 1:17). It is repeated on numerous occasions that "no one can see God and live" (Ex. 33:20, 1John 4:7, John 1:18, John 5:37), yet God is reported to have been seen on numerous occasions (Gen. 12:7, Gen. 17:1, Gen. 18:1, Gen. 26:2, Gen. 32:30, Ex. 3:16, Ex. 6:2-3, Ex. 24:9-11, Ex.33:11, Num. 12:7-8, Num. 14:14, Job 42:5, Amos 7:7-8, Amos 9:1). And of course, Christians believe Jesus (pbuh) was God, and he was seen by multitudes of people. Their belief is in spite of the fact that Jesus (pbuh) says no one has seen God or heard his voice at any time (John 5:37). Moses (pbuh) is said to have seen God's back part (Ex. 33:22-23). The Bible says that God is not a man that he should lie (Num. 23:19), but Jeremiah says that God deceived him (Jer. 20:7). It says that God is not the son of man that he should repent (Num. 23:19), yet God is reported to have repented on several occasions (Gen. 6:6, Ex. 32:14, Judges 2:18, 2Sam. 24:16, Jer. 26:19, Jon. 3:10). Repented to whom?

This is a good question. If repent means regret, then there still exists the idea that God made a mistake. God is not a man that he can be tempted of evil, and Jesus (pbuh) is considered to be God, yet he was tempted by the devil (Mark 1:12-13). Jacob (pbuh) wrestled a man, who turned out to be God (Gen. 32:24-30), for which he was renamed Israel, which means "wrestle with God" and he named the place where this match occurred Peniel, meaning "face of God." Jacob (pbuh) named this place Peniel because he saw "God face to face" and his life was preserved. Exodus 15:3 plainly states that "the Lord is a MAN of war." There is no doubt that these references and many more like them cause great confusion about God's nature. And it sets the groundwork for a man to be called God.

There are also hints of henotheism in the Old Testament, which is the devotion to one God, while acknowledging the existence of other gods. The first commandment could be cited as an example, which says "thou shall have no other Gods before me" (Ex. 20:3). Another example is Exodus 15:11 which says, "who is like thee, O Lord among the gods?" Psalms 82:6 makes mention of "gods" and God makes Moses a "god" to pharaoh (Ex. 7:1). These and other examples have been used to demonstrate that the Jews may have accepted other gods, but held the "God of Israel" to be their God and he was superior to the other gods. The

Israelites began to worship idols and false gods several times before their Babylonian captivity.

In Babylon the Jews were exposed to the Persian monotheistic religion, Zoroastrianism. After the Babylonian captivity, Jews became stricter in their view of monotheism and never again fell to the worship of false gods in the Old Testament. Monotheism is presented in a clearer form after this capture with statements like "I am the Lord and there is none else" (Isa. 45:18) or "I am God, and there is none else: I am God, and there is none like me" (Isa. 46:9). Thus we can conclude that the nature of God, as a spirit or a man and the existence of a multiplicity of gods and a singular God are not always crystal clear in the Old Testament. And in seeking to fulfill prophecies of the Old Testament, it is understandable how New Testament authors are enticed to make a mighty man of God into a mighty God.

What Was God's Purpose for Becoming a Man?

If someone were to ask a Christian, "why did God become a man?," they most likely will response with one of three answers or all three answers. The first and most important is that God came in the form of man to be a sacrifice and atonement for the Original Sin. And the second reason was to understand man and his struggles. The last reason was that Jesus (pbuh) came to set an example for mankind to follow.

This last reason can easily be disqualified because it is not necessary for God to be an example. There are many people in the Bible who God declares as righteous and sinless, as will be discussed in the section entitled "JESUS (pbuh) IS GOD BECAUSE HE WAS SINLESS?" The life of such people must be excellent examples to follow considering that God felt it necessary to pronounce his approval of their character. Though the Bible contains several details of prophet's lives which can be described as crude, sinful and utterly despicable, I am inclined to believe that God makes much more sound decisions when electing those who will carry out his mission. So I consider such tales of these prophets of God to be inaccurate, to say the least.

With that said, the prophets of God should be of the character that is adequate to be admired, followed and mimicked. Therefore, being an example is not exclusive to God. Actually Jesus (pbuh) followed the laws of Moses and as most Christians would say, Jesus (pbuh) is the fulfillment of a prophecy about a prophet to come who will be like Moses (pbuh) (Deut. 18:18). This would seem to mean that Moses (pbuh) must have had an impeccable character, in order for "God" to come to earth in his likeness. This accentuates the point made above and raises a new point. Was Moses (pbuh) God's example to follow? In fact, God as an example would be a hard act to follow, but if Jesus (pbuh) was God then he followed in Moses' (pbuh) footsteps.

The idea that God came down to earth to understand man's life is one which is embraced by Christians, but almost immediately recanted when put into perspective. The person who holds that Jesus (pbuh) came to understand man must confess that God knows everything. Therefore God should already know and understand man and his life.

In fact, he created man and every situation and circumstance that could possibly affect man's life.

To say that God must become a man to understand man is similar to saying I must become a robot to understand a robot, or I must become a radio to understand a radio. The inventor knows what he has made and he is able to explain every aspect of this invention. To a greater degree, God is the creator and he is all-knowing. He doesn't have to become a man to understand man.

The idea that God must come down to earth to see for himself finds its origin in the Old Testament, where God comes to talk to Moses (pbuh) (Ex. 33:11), or where God comes to Earth to see the Tower of Babel (Gen. 11:5). In the story of Adam (pbuh) and Eve's transgression in the Garden of Eden there is another example of God coming to see things for himself (Gen. 3:8). This notion that God needed to understand man is another candidate for deletion as a reason for God to come to earth.

The remaining response is that God came to earth as the man named Jesus (pbuh) to take on the sin of the world. I have dealt with this topic extensively in my book entitled "Jesus (pbuh) Was Not Crucified." In that book, the doctrine of sin and atonement in Christianity are explained. So it is unnecessary to go into great detail to denounce the idea that Jesus (pbuh) died to absolve man from the punishment of sin. What you will find is that their doctrines of Original Sin and Atonement, just like the doctrine of the Trinity, were established long after Jesus' (pbuh) lifetime. And the gist of my argument against the Christian viewpoint is articulated perfectly in the Book of Ezekiel (pbuh) in the Bible.

Ezekiel 18:20 *The soul that sinneth, it shall die; the son shall not bear the iniquity of the father with him, neither shall the father bear the iniquity of the son with him; the righteousness of the righteous shall be upon him, and the wickedness of the wicked shall be upon him.*
Ezekiel 18:21 *But if the wicked turn from all his sins that he hath committed, and keep all My statutes, and do that which is lawful and right, he shall surely live, he shall not die.*
Ezekiel 18:22 *None of his transgressions that he hath committed shall be remembered against him; for his righteousness that he hath done he shall live.*

When reading through these verses, we find that sin is not inherited as the Christian doctrine of the Original Sin suggests. Thus each person is held accountable for their own sin, not some innocent person or God. Also, these verses suggest that man is capable of vindicating himself by his own actions of repentance and righteousness. God punishes only the guilty party and he forgives man without sacrificing an innocent man. The guilty bear their own burden and their salvation into heaven is based upon their ability to eschew their wickedness and do what is righteous. So, we find that there is no legitimate reason for God to become a man. God could overcome each of these supposed obstacles without becoming a man.

My favorite movie is "BRAVEHEART." In the scene in which Mel Gibson is introducing himself to the troops, several of the troops suppose that he is not truly William Wallace, the leader of the rebellion against England. They all have heard fantastic stories that Wallace is seven feet tall and he kills his enemies by the hundreds. This exaggerated legend is given life because of the tremendous feats achieved by Wallace on the battlefield to free an oppressed people. William Wallace killed people and he is made into a giant. Jesus (pbuh) healed people, in order for those around to hear his message. Just imagine the stories generated around this man. These stories became more exaggerated until Jesus (pbuh) was given the ultimate status.

Gary Miller, a former Christian theologian, suggests that the idea of Jesus (pbuh) being God came about when the focal point became the messenger instead of the message. Miller insists that this fixation on the person delivering the message caused writers to compete on who could write the best stories about this particular person. And the stories become more and more exaggerated, until the person is deified. Perhaps this is why there were so many gospels written. Could those which were lost or destroyed have contained a less than divine Jesus (pbuh), thus giving cause for their extinction? We may never know.

One other point to mention is that God's presence on earth would make the people, he came to, feel quite superior to others. Though the pictures of Jesus (pbuh) in churches all over the world are all total fabrications and most everyone knows this fact, no one has made an effort to rectify this. In the region in which Jesus (pbuh) lived, the people had no resemblance to these pictures. However every year a movie comes out about Jesus (pbuh) and he is portrayed as a white Anglo-Saxon. This is a root cause for racism.

If God was white, it is easy to surmise that the white race is superior to the other races. In addition to this, the rulers of much of the world are white men, giving non-whites the impression that God favors them over others. Not to be outdone, black people have laid claim to Jesus (pbuh) as being of their persuasion. This too is an unhealthy approach because they are ingrained with the same superiority complex. This idea of God becoming a man seems to always include God become a man that looks like the person narrating the story. It instills racial pride, but harbors the idea of racial superiority. Because of such a problem, God would not become a man.

PLURALS

One of the most misunderstood and misinterpreted aspects of the Hebrew Scriptures, which is used as a proof of the Trinity, is the plural nouns and pronouns used for God. For example, the Bible reads that God said "Let US make man in OUR image" (Gen. 1:26). Trinitarians suggest that this is inferring the presence of the Father, Son and Holy Spirit. But Judaism is a very strict monotheistic religion, which does not have a belief in Jesus (pbuh) as a prophet of God, and definitely not God. So how do Jews reconcile this issue?

Did the Trinitarians consult any Jews as to what their scriptures meant by the plurals? It is inconceivable that they never mentioned this to the Jews, considering Christians' zeal for evangelism. It would be unfathomable for a Christian preacher or evangelist not to capitalize on the crystal clear evidence of a different understanding of the unity of God. Perhaps they did ask and the answer was unsatisfactory in their minds and they preached this plural as evidence of the Trinity despite the knowledge of the Hebrew language's pluralis majestatis. Pluralis majestatis (majestic plural) is the plural pronoun which refers to one person alone. This is also known as the "royal we" or the "Victorian we." These plurals are used to demonstrate someone's royalty, sovereignty and might. It is used for kings and queens. For example, a person comes before the king to entertain him but he is unsuccessful and the king says "We are not amused."

In light of the fact that God is most noble, most royal, most sovereign and Almighty, he is most deserving of this plural of respect. Also, the word used for God in the Hebrew Scriptures, Elohim, is plural. Therefore a Trinitarian who insists that the "we" and "us" are plurals of numbers must complete this understanding and have Elohim translated as "gods." Of course, they will not do this because this change would indicate polytheism, a claim which they vehemently deny.

English is one of the few languages which don't have this majestic plural, but its presence did impact modern English. At one point the word "you" had the distinction of being used only for plurals and "thou" was used for singularity. But the pluralis majestatis, also called "T-V distinction," of France influenced modern English to discontinue the distinction between the plural and singular forms for you. "You" is now singular and plural.

Another language which uses this plural of respect is Arabic, which is a language very similar to Hebrew. In the Qur'an, God is mentioned using plurals, also. And just as every Hebrew speaking person knows that this plural in no way compromised the oneness of God, nor articulates a notion of the Trinity, no Arabic speaking person (including Arab Christians) would contend that the Qur'an gives any support to a Trinity or anything other than strict monotheism.

Though Muhammad (pbuh) was contested on many issues, no one, including the Arab polytheists, ever accused him of believing in more than one God. This claim by Trinitarians to support its doctrine is unfounded and should be denounced by every honest Bible translator, Bible scholar, and Christian minister.

PART IV

THE REFUTATION OF THE EVIDENCE THAT JESUS (PBUH) IS GOD

JESUS (PBUH) THE SON OF GOD

Jesus (pbuh) is called the son of Joseph in Luke 3:23, even though Mary was supposed to be a virgin. The translators add in parentheses, the words "as was supposed" to illustrate that this was the common belief of the people who knew the family. It is odd that the Bible, which is believed to be inspired by God, includes Joseph in the genealogy of Jesus (pbuh) on two occasions, but it never includes God as Jesus' (pbuh) father. Jesus (pbuh) is also called the son of Adam (pbuh), the son of David (pbuh) and the Son of Abraham (pbuh) (Matt. 1:1) and all of these are understood to be metaphorical. But when he is called the son of God, it becomes literal. Trinitarians take "son of God" literally, when it is a Jewish idiom like "let the dead bury the dead", "be born again" and "pick up your cross and follow me." These are figures of speech and they are not to be taken literally. So too is "Son of God." It is also a figure of speech.

The sonship of Jesus (pbuh) is a huge obstacle to hurdle in pursuit of the truth. Jesus (pbuh) is described as the Son of Man and the Son of God in the Gospels. It is of popular belief that "Son of Man" is in reference to his humanity, as a son of a man is a man. But "Son of God" gives rise to the claim of Jesus' (pbuh) divinity as God. I would suggest that the aforementioned, "Son of Man" is in reference to his humanity. And it was a tool used to ensure that people did not misunderstand this miraculous man's life and consider him to be God or take the words "son of God" literally. In the book of Job (pbuh), the difference between God, man and the Son of Man is expressed in clear terms.

Job 25:4 *How then can man be just with God? Or how can he be clean that is born of a woman?*
Job 25:5 *Behold, even the moon hath no brightness, and the*
stars are not pure in His sight;
Job 25:6 *How much less man, that is a worm! and the son of*
man, that is a maggot!

These verses seem to indicate that a man born of a woman is unqualified to even be considered as a comparison to God. Not only that but it seems that the Son of Man is inferior to the man himself, according to your perspective on worms and maggots, of course. Nonetheless, the author is giving his views that the Son of Man is less pure than man. If we insert Jesus (pbuh) into this verse because he was born of a woman and he is entitled the Son of Man, it can be concluded by these verses that he is incomparable to God. Also, the title Son of Man was not a title given exclusively to Jesus (pbuh). Ezekiel (pbuh) was on several occasions in the Bible called Son of Man. In like manner, there are a multitude of people in the Bible called Son of God.

Genesis 6:2 *That the sons of God saw the daughters of men that they were fair; and they took them wives of all which they chose.*

Psalms 82:6 *I have said, Ye are gods; and all of you are all children of the most High.*

2Samuel 7:14 *I will be his father, and he shall be my son*

Psalms 89:26 *He shall cry unto me, Thou [art] my father, my God, and the rock of my salvation*
Psalms 89:27 *Also I will make him [my] firstborn, higher than the kings of the earth.*

Exodus 4:22 *And thou shalt say unto Pharaoh, Thus saith the LORD, Israel [is] my son, [even] my firstborn:*

Jeremiah 31:9 *for I am a father to Israel, and Ephraim is my firstborn.*

It is of a certainty that no Christian on Earth believes every instance in which they read that someone is the son of God, that the subject is therefore God in human form. They will proclaim that this "son of God" is figurative, but Jesus (pbuh) was literally God's son. However, "son of God" cannot be literal, because they are contradictory terms. The son of a monkey is a monkey. The son of a bee is a bee. And the son of God is God. But a "son" is by definition someone who receives life from his parents. In sharp contrast, God is someone who doesn't receive life from anyone. So, Jesus (pbuh) can't receive life and not receive life. A son cannot be God and God cannot be someone's son. Nonetheless, Jesus (pbuh) is still called the only

"Begotten" son of God. For some Trinitarians this must be the case because it is apparent that he was not God's only son. So what does this word "begotten" mean?

As stated earlier it means to father, to sire or to produce. In debate, one may say that begotten means to produce, not to father. However God produced everyone, especially Adam (pbuh). So it can't be said that Jesus (pbuh) was the "only Produced" Son of God. Also, the Athanasian Creed explicitly says Jesus (pbuh) is not made or created, but begotten. This deduction leaves Christians with the meaning in which the Nicea Creed alluded to, to father or sire. However this word, "begotten" brings about huge criticism from non-Christians, more specifically the Muslim. A Muslim is incensed by the idea that God fathered or sired a human being in any way. The Quran asked:

Al-Quran 6:101 *"How can He (Allah) have a son, when He does not even have a wife?"*

This begs the moral question of an actual father and son without an actual mother. This is not the ideal family in any civilized society, let alone Christian society. This dilemma led Catholics into what Protestants believe to be the deification of Mary, as the mother of God. But are they wrong? The Council of Ephesus in 431 declared that Mary is "Theotokos," The Mother of God because she gave birth not to a man but God as a man. Most Protestants believe Jesus (pbuh) to be God. Who was Jesus' (pbuh) mother? Mary. Therefore she was the mother of God and she should be held in high esteem for her position, if he is actually God. The word "begotten" correlates to the act used to produce a child by a man, just as "conceived" is the description of a woman's actions in this process. This picture is painted in your mind when Luke describes the angel and Mary's conversation about the birth of Jesus (pbuh).

Luke 1:35 *The angel answered, "The Holy Spirit will come upon you, and the power of the Most High will overshadow you. So the holy one to be born will be called the Son of God.*

Christians have pointed out that the Nicean Creed says that Jesus (pbuh) was "begotten before all the worlds" and it reiterates the Athanasian Creed, that he was "begotten not made." They say that this shows that begotten isn't to be taken literally because no one was with God, not even Mary. Yet it still says that God fathered Jesus (pbuh). The famous question Christians pose is "Since Jesus (pbuh) had no father, who was his father?" The answer is in the question, he had no father. A counter question might be "How did God father Jesus (pbuh), without a mother?"

Though both are paradoxical questions, they have the same answer, if you think about it. It was as the Bible says a miraculous birth without a father. There have been some people who conclude that Jesus (pbuh) is literally God's son because he was born miraculously without a father. This is easily contested by the story of Adam (pbuh) and Melchizedek, both of whom had no mother or father (Gen.2:7, Heb. 7:3). By the standard proposed, Adam (pbuh) and Melchizedek are better candidates for divinity, yet no one is willing to nominate them.

In the search for the meaning of the word "begotten" as it is used in the Bible, we find that the author of Psalms, traditional known as David was also called the "only begotten son of god" (Psalms 2:7). What does this say for this title when it is given to Jesus (pbuh)? How can two people be the "only one?" The word appears again in the book of Hebrews with reference to Isaac (pbuh). The parallel is being drawn between Abraham's (pbuh) sacrificing of his son and that of the Father's sacrifice of his Son, Jesus (pbuh).

Hebrews 11:17 *By faith Abraham, when he was tried, offered up Isaac: and he that had received the promises offered up his only begotten son.*

Of course, Isaac (pbuh) was never Abraham's (pbuh) only begotten son, because his brother, Ishmael (pbuh), was born before him (Gen. 16:15, Gen. 21:3) meaning Ishmael (pbuh) is the only child who could have been called the only begotten. With recent developments it has been found that "begotten" is not the correct translation of the Greek term used in the text.

Modern translations use "unique Son," "only Son," or something similar because the second root-word of μσυογενής is understood to be γενοζ (kind, type) rather than γεννάω (to beget, to father). Thus it should read "only + kind" rather than "only + begotten."

The passages containing "only begotten" like John 3:16 and Hebrews 11:17, now reads "only son" or "one and only son" in most Bibles, yet the prolific King James Version still contains "only begotten."

Actually this most famous verse of the Bible John 3:16-21 is considered by some Bible scholars to be an interpolation and they end the quote at John 3:15. That withstanding, the problems of the word "begotten" are obvious. So too, are the alternative of "one and only" son. In the Bible, neither Jesus (pbuh) nor Isaac (pbuh) was the one and only sons. Isaac (pbuh) is also called the only son at the sacrifice, even though Ishmael (pbuh) is called Abraham's (pbuh) son throughout Abraham's (pbuh) life and at his death. Thus it is not presumptuous to conclude that "one and only son" or "only begotten son" are auspicious terms used to annunciate the Bible author's and the most popular view of these figures. This idea rings true when we consider what Jesus (pbuh) said to Mary Magdalene in John.

John 20:17 *Jesus saith unto her, Touch me not; for I am not yet ascended to my Father: but go to my brethren, and say unto them, I ascend unto my Father, and your Father; and [to] my God, and your God.*

It is clear in this verse that Jesus' (pbuh) understanding of the Father is one who is a father to all equally. In the book of Matthew, Jesus (pbuh) tells the multitudes of their Father (God) time after time. Also Jesus (pbuh) commands his followers to start their prayers with the words "Our Father" (Matt. 6:9, Luke 11:3). These verses show Jesus (pbuh) making no distinction between his sonship of God and his followers. This seems to contradiction the notion of Jesus' (pbuh) uniqueness as God's son. The Aramaic word "abba" or FATHER used by Jesus (pbuh) in Mark 14:36 is to be used by all Christians according to Galatians 4:6.

Along the same lines, we find that verses are completely fabricated to proclaim Jesus (pbuh) as the son of God. The earliest and most reliable manuscripts of the Gospel of Mark have no record of the words "son of God" in the very first statement of the first chapter. When it is printed in the Bible, it will usually have a footnote or parenthesis around it to indicate that it is an interpolation. In Acts chapter 8, we find the testimony of Philip about Jesus (pbuh). Chapter 8:37 records Philip proclaiming to believe that "Jesus is the Son of God." However, this verse is not authentic and it is followed by some form of reference to this fact, with an asterisk, a letter or a number for the reader to refer to the footnotes.

Acts 9:20 *And straightway he (Paul) preached Christ in the synagogues, that he is the Son of God.*

It seems that Paul is responsible for calling Jesus (pbuh) the son of God. And the writers of the gospels followed suit, attempting to make "the son of God" have more meaning when it pertains to Jesus (pbuh). The parable of the "Husbandman" is a clear example of this (Matt. 21:33-46, Mark 12:1-12, Luke 20:9-19).

This parable distinguishes Jesus (pbuh) as someone, not simply sent by God, but God's son who must be killed. I believe this parable to be an invention attributed to Jesus, mainly due to the fact that Jesus (pbuh) was not killed according to the Bible. This is a topic discussed in the "RESURRECTION" section briefly, yet sufficiently (I have dealt with the topic in more detail in my book entitled "Jesus (pbuh) Was Not Crucified"). If it can be shown that Jesus (pbuh) did not die, it will be obvious that this parable is another attempt to portray Jesus (pbuh) in the light that they wished him to be seen in and not the light he portrayed.

With a small study of the gospel accounts, we find that John, Luke and Mark can't hold a candle to Matthew when it comes to furthering Paul's agenda. With a simple comparison of the gospels where the same story is told, Matthew's intentions shine bright. He adds the words "Son of God" or "Father" to the text or he alters the words to incorporate his message.

{Example 1}
Mark 15:29 *And they that passed by railed on him, wagging their heads, and saying, Ah, thou that destroyest the temple, and buildest it in three days,*
Mark 15:30 *Save thyself, and come down from the cross.*

Matthew 27:40 *And saying, Thou that destroyest the temple, and buildest it in three days, save thyself. If thou be the Son of God, come down from the cross.*

{Example 2}
Mark 6:51 *And he went up unto them into the ship; and the wind ceased: and they were sore amazed in themselves beyond measure, and wondered.*
Mark 6:52 *For they considered not the miracle of the loaves: for their heart was hardened.*

Matthew 14:32 *And when they were come into the ship, the wind ceased.*
Matthew 14:33 *Then they that were in the ship came and worshipped him, saying, Of a truth thou art the Son of God.*

{Example 3}
Mark 8:29 *And he saith unto them, But whom say ye that I am? And Peter answereth and saith unto him, Thou art the Christ.*
Luke 9:20 *He said unto them, But whom say ye that I am? Peter answering said, The Christ of God.*

Matthew 16:16 *And Simon Peter answered and said, Thou art the Christ, the Son of the living God.*

{Example 4}
Luke 12:6 *Are not five sparrows sold for two farthings, and not one of them is forgotten before God?*

Matthew 10:29 *Are not two sparrows sold for a farthing? and one of them shall not fall on the ground without your Father.*

{Example 5}
Luke 12:8 *Also I say unto you, Whosoever shall confess me before men, him shall the Son of man also confess before the angels of God:*
Luke 12:9 *But he that denieth me before men shall be denied before the angels of God.*

Matthew 10:32 *Whosoever therefore shall confess me before men, him will I confess also before my Father which is in heaven.*
Matthew 10:33 *But whosoever shall deny me before men, him will I also deny before my Father which is in heaven.*

{Example 6}
Mark 3:35 *For whosoever shall do the will of God, the same is my brother, and my sister, and mother.*

Luke 8:21 *And he answered and said unto them, My mother and my brethren are these which hear the word of God, and do it.*

Matthew 12:50 *For whosoever shall do the will of my Father which is in heaven, the same is my brother, and sister, and mother.*

I would ask you to consider the reason that such additions or substitutions would be necessary. Could it be to convey a certain message to the reader, perhaps that Jesus was the literal Son of God?

So what is the definition of the phrase "Son of God?" Who better to define the phrase than Jesus (pbuh)? On one occasion, Jesus (pbuh) said whoever accepts and follows him is the son of God (John 1:12). He also said, "Blessed are the peacemakers, for they will be called sons of God (Matt. 5:9)." For the sake of argument, the fact that this man called "the Prince of Peace" declared on two separate occasions that he did not come for peace (Matt. 10:34, Luke 12:51), thus disqualifying him from being a son of God, will be disregarded. Instead, let's consider the centurion at the cross with Jesus (pbuh).

In the Gospels of Matthew (27:54) and Mark (15:39), the centurion is reported to have said "Truly this man was the Son of God." Yet Luke, who is considered by Bible scholars to be the most reliable and accurate of the gospels, reports that the centurion said "Certainly this was a righteous man (23:47). This would have the reader to believe that "a righteous man" and "the son of God" are synonymous and interchangeable terms. Paul affirms this notion when he says:

Romans 8:14 *For as many as are led by the Spirit of God, they are the sons of God.*

If we take all of these definitions into consideration, we see that a son of God is a righteous person, a peacemaker, who is led by the Spirit of God and accepts and follows God's prophets. To cement this understanding of the son of God, we can look again at the words of Jesus (pbuh). When in confrontation with his detractors, Jesus (pbuh) said God is his Father and the Jews, whom he was speaking with, were fathered by the devil.

John 8:42 *Jesus said unto them, If God were your Father, ye would love me: for I proceeded forth and came from God; neither came I of myself, but he sent me.*
John 8:43 *Why do ye not understand my speech? [even] because ye cannot hear my word.*
John 8:44 *Ye are of [your] father the devil*

The first point to be made is that Jesus (pbuh) is calling the Father God. This again shows that the Bible and Jesus (pbuh) have proclaimed the Father to be God, yet neither says that the son is God. The second point is that Jesus (pbuh) says that he "proceeded from the Father." However in the Athanasian Creed the Holy Spirit is the person said to "proceed" from the Father, whereas Jesus was "begotten" by the Father. The words are used specifically for each person. This means the creed and the words of Jesus (pbuh) are in contrast to each other. But the third and most important point was Jesus' (pbuh) usage of the word "father" for the devil. Did he really believe the devil fathered or produced the people that he was speaking to? Was he figuratively or literally speaking? The answer is that he is speaking figuratively. He meant that these were sinful people following the oath of the devil. So we must assume that when he described himself as the son of God in this very same instance, he meant it figuratively as a righteous person following the path set by God. But what about the instance when the high priest questioned Jesus (pbuh) about being the son of the Blessed One?

Mark 14:61 *But he was silent and answered nothing. Again the high priest asked him and said to him, "Are you the Messiah, the son of the Blessed One?"*
Mark 14:62 *Then Jesus answered, "I am; and 'you will see the Son of Man seated at the right hand of the Power and coming with the clouds of heaven.'"*

Though we now see that Jesus' (pbuh) mentioning of the son of God was figurative, let's examine the above verse more closely.

Perhaps, because the word God is replaced with "Blessed One," some might give this answer more weight towards proving Jesus' (pbuh) divinity. When asked, was he the Christ and the son of God, Jesus (pbuh) says yes but he exchanges "son of God" with "son of man." The significance of this is that Jesus (pbuh) sees no distinction between the two, whereas Trinitarians say these are two natures of Jesus (pbuh). Jesus (pbuh) also, says that the "son of man", the one believed to be the human side of Jesus (pbuh), will be in heaven, not the divinely natured Jesus (pbuh). But this is only one of the synoptic Gospels, what does the other gospels say of this question and answer session? The answer may surprise you.

Matthew 26:63 *But Jesus held his peace. And the high priest answered and said unto him, I adjure thee by the living God, that thou tell us whether thou be the Christ, the Son of God,*
Matthew 26:64 *Jesus saith unto him, Thou hast said: nevertheless I say unto you, Hereafter shall ye see the Son of man sitting on the right hand of power, and coming in the clouds of heaven.*

Along with the different wording of the question, Jesus' (pbuh) answer is also completely different in Matthew. Jesus (pbuh) does not say answer, "yes, I am." His reply to the question, "is he the Messiah, the son of God?" is "that's what you say" or "you say that." So, Jesus (pbuh) did not answer the questions at all. A few Bibles replace "thou hast said" with "yes" or "I am He" in the verses of Matthew to coincide with Mark. This again is dishonest translation because succeeding the phrase in questions is the word "nevertheless" or "but," which indicate a positive coming from a negative or neutral answer. In other words, if he actually acknowledged that he was the son of God, he would have said, yes I am "and" I will be coming in the clouds, not yes I am, "but" I will be coming in the clouds.

Mark's account uses "and," not "but" or "nevertheless," because with this answer, it makes sense. So, again Matthew's account is conflicting with Mark's gospel. If Matthew's version is accurate then Mark's rendition should not be used to prove that Jesus (pbuh) is the son of God. But what about the other synoptic gospel whose author seeks to make an accurate and orderly account of Jesus' (pbuh) life. Luke comes to both Mark's and Matthew's rescue, as well as those seeking the truth.

Luke 22:66 *And as soon as it was day, the elders of the people and the chief priests and the scribes came together, and led him into their council, saying,*
Luke 22:67 *Art thou the Christ? tell us. And he said unto them, If I tell you, ye will not believe:*
Luke 22:68 *And if I also ask [you], ye will not answer me, nor let [me] go.*
Luke 22:69 *Hereafter shall the Son of man sit on the right hand of the power of God.*
Luke 22:70 *Then said they all, Art thou then the Son of God? And he said unto them, Ye say that I am.*

Luke helps clarify this story, which Mark and Matthew have mystified. Luke shows that the questions and answers are separated. First the high priest, the elders and the scribes, all asks Jesus (pbuh), "is he the Christ?" Jesus (pbuh) does not answer them, but he replies that they wouldn't believe his answer. He then speaks of the Son of Man on the right hand of the power of God. After this, they asked Jesus (pbuh), "is he the son of God?"

From Luke, we find that Mark and Matthew were both partially right. Matthew says "you say that" and Mark says "I am," but Jesus (pbuh) actually says "you say that I am." These three stories can be expounded upon from several angles, but for this book it is important to note that in this line of questioning, Jesus (pbuh) did not say he was the Messiah or the son of God. So this event cannot be honestly used to prove that Jesus (pbuh) said he was God's son.

The gospel of John uses a more vague line of questioning about Jesus (pbuh) teachings, which makes no reference to Jesus (pbuh) being the son of God. And Jesus (pbuh) doesn't answer in John either. He tells the high priest to asks the people who heard his message for the answer (John 18:19-21). This should disqualify the use of Mark 14:61-62 in any debate about the sonship of Jesus (pbuh).

And finally, it is in bad company that the Trinitarians find themselves in, when they assert that Jesus (pbuh) is God because he says God is his Father.

John 5:17 *But Jesus answered them, My Father worketh hitherto, and I work.*
John 5:18 *Therefore the Jews sought the more to kill him, because he not only had broken the sabbath, but said also that God was his Father, making himself equal with God.*

The enemies of Jesus (pbuh) believed that Jesus (pbuh) was proclaiming his divinity by saying "My Father." Those who believe in the Trinity say that Jesus' (pbuh) enemies understood him correctly. The major problem with this claim is that whenever the Jews accused Jesus (pbuh) of blasphemy, Jesus (pbuh) corrected their misunderstanding. He reaffirmed time and time again that "son of God" is not to be taken literally. He never ever said, "You are right. I am making myself equal to God." On the contrary, he says that he is powerless without God and God has taught him everything that he knows. Someone who is given power and given understanding is not God.

John 5:19 *Then answered Jesus and said unto them, Verily, verily, I say unto you, The Son can do nothing of* *himself, but what he seeth the Father do: for what things soever he doeth, these also doeth the Son likewise.*

MESSIAH IS GOD?

Matthew 16:15 *He said to them, "But who do you say that I am?"*
Matthew 16:16 *Simon Peter said in reply, "You are the Messiah, the Son of the living God."*
Matthew 16:17 *Jesus said to him in reply, "Blessed are you, Simon son of Jonah. For flesh and blood has not revealed this to you, but my heavenly Father.*
Matthew 16:18 *And so I say to you, you are Peter, and upon this rock I will build my church, and the gates of the netherworld shall not prevail against it.*
Matthew 16:19 *I will give you the keys to the kingdom of heaven. Whatever you bind on earth shall be bound in heaven; and whatever you loose on earth shall be loosed in heaven."*
Matthew 16:20 *Then he strictly ordered his disciples to tell no one that he was the Messiah.*

What is the definition of the word Messiah? Messiah (mese_é) or Messias (mese_és) literally means anointed. The Greek word for anointed is Christos, which is now translated into English as Christ. This word has been misunderstood to denote "God" or "the literal son of God." The Hebrew word for Messiah and its derivatives appear several times in the Bible, yet it is only translated Christ when it applies to Jesus (pbuh). Tabernacles were anointed with oil (Lev. 8:10), pillars were anointed with oil (Gen. 31:13) and Jesus (pbuh) anointed the eyes of a blind man with clay (John 9:6). As done in present day, those appointed to high offices go through a ceremony to consecrate their position.

Priests (Leviticus 4:3) and cherubs (Ezekiel 28:14) were anointed in the Bible. David (1Samuel 16:13), Solomon (1King 1:39), and Saul (1Sam. 9:16-17) were anointed. From these examples, it is clear that "God" or "Son of God" is not even implied and that the translators are making it appear that "Messiah" is only used for Jesus (pbuh). And what is interesting is in Isaiah we find another Messiah.

Isaiah 45:1 *Thus says the LORD to Cyrus His anointed.*

This seems to be a clear form of deceit used by the translators. If ever there was a case for the use of the word "Christ" for someone or something other than Jesus (pbuh) it is here. The Lord himself anointed and appointed this pagan king to deliver Israel. The problem is there can't be two Christs, because Christians take Christ to mean someone divine and no divinity is given to Cyrus. But the title Messiah or Christ is not a term used to place divinity on its subject. It is simply someone specially appointed to do a job. If you notice, the titles "messiah" and "son of God" are used to complement each other. Simon Peter (Matt. 16:17), Martha (John 11:27) and the high priest (Matt 26:63), and the author of John (20:31), all use these titles together when describing Jesus (pbuh). Thus Jesus (pbuh) was a righteous man specially appointed by God to deliver a message or the Messiah, the son of God.

The Jews never thought the Messiah was going to be God in human form, but rather a deliverer and king of Israel. It has been claimed that because the Jews accused Jesus (pbuh) of blasphemy for declaring himself to be the Messiah, that it is obvious that they understood that the Messiah will be God. The Jews didn't believe Jesus (pbuh) to be the Messiah, but the reason that they rejected Jesus (pbuh) was because he spoke of victory in Heaven, when the Jews wanted victory on earth from the oppressive Roman Empire. So they deduced that Jesus (pbuh) was an imposter and a false messiah. His blasphemy was not that he claimed to be God by saying that he was the Messiah. They asserted that his blasphemy was lying in God's name about his appointed position.

IN THE NAME OF JESUS (PBUH)

Matthew 1:21 *And she shall bring forth a son, and thou shalt call his name JESUS: for he shall save his people from their sins.*

Jesus' (pbuh) name means God saves. Some suggests that this is in some way a pronunciation of the divinity of Jesus (pbuh). The presence of the word God in the meaning of a person's name does not grant that person divinity. If that were the case then there have been millions of Gods on the earth. In the Bible alone we have Israel, Ishmael (pbuh), Gabriel (pbuh), Ezekiel (pbuh), and so on. But to narrow things down a bit, the actual name Jesus was not first given to the son born to Mary. The name Jesus was as it is today a very popular name. Of course, the name "Jesus" is Latinized, but in fact it is the Greek form of the Hebrew name Joshua. Of course, Joshua is the same name of the successor to Moses (pbuh), yet no one claims that Joshua is God.

Nor does anyone consider Bar Jesus (Acts 15:6), or Jesus Justus (Col. 4:11) to be God.

SAVIOR IS GOD?

Jesus (pbuh) is called the Savior. This alone is not indicative of the Trinitarians' claim of his divinity. But the fact that God is called the Savior (Isaiah 43:3) and he declares that there is no other Savior beside him (Isaiah 43:11) gives some the impulse to proclaim Jesus' (pbuh) equality to God. Passages like Titus 1:34 cause some people's head to spin when they are compared to the words of God in Isaiah.

Titus 1:3 *...according to the commandment of God our Savior,*
Titus 1:4 *To Titus, my true child in a common faith: Grace and peace from God the Father and Christ Jesus our Savior.*

But does this phenomenon only occur with regard to Jesus (pbuh)? Not at all. The translators of the Bible would have the reader believe that Jesus (pbuh) is the only other Savior mentioned in the Bible. The same Hebrew word, moh·shi´a' (meaning savior, deliverer or redeemer) that is used in Isaiah 43:11 is applied to Othniel, a judge in Israel, but Othniel is not consider to be God. It is no surprise that the translators of the popular King James Version contain the words "deliverer" instead of "savior" to keep his charade going. The same word is translated "savior" for God and Jesus (pbuh) and "deliverer" for Othniel.

Judges 3:9 *And when the children of Israel cried unto the LORD, the LORD raised up a deliverer to the children of*

Israel, who delivered them, even Othniel the son of Kenaz, Caleb's younger brother.

In 2Kings 13:5, God sends Israel a deliverer, King Jehoahaz. And the Bible mentions "saviors" in Nehemiah 9:27 and Obadiah 1:21. But how does one reconcile the numerous saviors and Isaiah 43:11, where God says that he is the only Savior. The book of Jude has our answer.

Jude 1:25 *To the only God our Savior, through Jesus Christ our Lord, let us give glory and honour and authority and power, before all time and now and for ever. So be it.*

The word "through" here is very important. It indicates that Jesus (pbuh) is but a vessel to bring about salvation. This verse is saying that God is the savior ultimately because he is responsible for sending the Saviors. It's like saying a general won the war. Even though he may not have fought in one battle, he orchestrated the battles. Therefore Jesus (pbuh) is a savior in the same sense that Jehoahaz and Othniel were. All three were tool used by God to save people.

When researching Jude 1:25, the reader may not find it in his King James Version. This is because the authors of the King James Version are content with the version stating:

"To the only wise God our Savior, be glory and majesty, dominion and power, both now and ever. Amen. (KJV)"

The oldest manuscripts of the Bible disagree with the King James Version on this verse. This has forced Biblical scholars to declare that the King James Version of Jude 1:25

to be a later substitution and corruption of the original text. It is apparent that some authors wish to ignore these findings in order to maintain that Jesus (pbuh) is the only savior. And because the majority of Christians subscribe to this notion, it becomes more convenient to cater to their needs than to tell the truth.

LORD IS GOD?

If you notice, there seems to be a trend starting. That is, every title given to Jesus (pbuh) has been taken literally, whereas the exact same term is used for others and it is understood to be metaphorical. For example, God is one definition of the word "lord" but it is most certainly not the only definition. The most popular use of the word, lord, is in reference to "A man of high rank in a feudal society or in one that retains feudal forms and institutions, especially." There is also the "general masculine title of nobility" and "a man with renowned power and authority." These selections are used to demonstrate that the word "lord" could be mistaken to mean something that the speaker did not intend for it to mean. The usage of capital letters, which is foreign to the languages of Greek, Hebrew and Aramaic, is a particular culprit in this misunderstanding, but it is not the sole problem.

I have suggested that the idea that Jesus (pbuh) was God has influenced translators to translate words like "savior" and "messiah" for Jesus (pbuh) and "deliverer" and "anointed" for others. They have also use capital letters for titles of Jesus (pbuh), but use lower case letters for others. This influences the reader immediately, because it reinforces the doctrine taught in the church. So from the start, the readers are spoon fed Jesus' (pbuh) divinity. And when you are fed information in this manner, it is easy to understand the doctrine the way in which it is taught, not necessarily the way in which it is actually written.

Is any other person called "lord" in the Bible? Of course. Abraham (pbuh) (Gen. 18:16) , Esau (Gen. 32:4), Potiphar (Gen. 39:16), Joseph (pbuh) (Gen. 44:20), and David (pbuh) (1Sam. 25:24) were all called "lord", but with a lower case "l" to help convey the message that they aren't "lord" like Jesus (pbuh) is "Lord." What is interesting is one verse used to declare Jesus' (pbuh) divinity, in fact, helps prove my claim that he was a man of high ranking, not God. David (pbuh) says

Mark 12:36 *"The Lord said to my Lord, "Sit at my right hand until I place your enemies under your feet."*

In this verse, there are two different ranks of "lords" present. The Lord is God and my Lord is understood to be Jesus (pbuh). The first lord is higher in stature than the second lord, similar to "The President (of the U.S.) said to my President (of ACME)." It can be argued that there could be lords or presidents of the same stature at the same company, but in the case of David (pbuh), if Jesus (pbuh) is understood to be God, then both lords would be his lord and the verse would read "My Lord said to my Lord."

To further illustrate this point, the words spoken by The Lord indicate that David's (pbuh) lord is to be THE Lord's right hand man. This brings to mind the title "Lord of Lords" given to Jesus (pbuh) (Rev 19:16). The phrase "Lord of Lords" in regards to Jesus (pbuh) must mean that he is the highest authority and power on earth, because he is still subject to the greatest Lord. Jude 1:4 echoes this very sentiment when it mentions the "only Lord God and our Lord Jesus." Also, if the title "lord" meant God, then why were those who called Jesus (pbuh) "lord," Jews (his disciples and followers) and non-Jews (the Canaanite woman and the centurion), not accused of blasphemy? Why was Jesus (pbuh) not accused of accepting a title which is blasphemous? Because the word was harmless. It is erroneous to give "lord" referring to Jesus (pbuh) a capital "L" and automatically equate Jesus (pbuh) with God. Nebuchadnezzar is called "king of kings" (Dan. 2:37) and the disciples are called the "light of the world" (Matt. 5:14) just as Jesus (pbuh) is (Rev. 17:14, John 8:12), but no one equates any of these individuals with Jesus (pbuh). In like manner, Jesus (pbuh) should not be equated with God. If the addition of capital letters were implemented in the cases of Nebuchadnezzar and the disciples, it would show how easily the author can convey his or her own viewpoint to the reader with a slight gesture.

The problem of "Lord" will arise again in regards to Doubting Thomas and it may be surprising!!!!

IMMANUEL

Isaiah 7:14 *Therefore the Lord himself shall give you a sign; Behold, a virgin shall conceive, and bear a son, and shall call his name Immanuel.*

Trinitarians have used this verse on numerous occasions to say that Jesus (pbuh) is Immanuel, which means "god with us." But it is one thing to say, "His name is God" and quite another to say, "He is God," especially considering that the Bible is filled with people with God in their names. And none of them are literally considered to be God. For example, God heard and answered the prayers of Abraham (pbuh) in the Bible and he had a son named Ishmael (pbuh), meaning God hears (prayers). But most assuredly, he is not God or God's actual hearing. And there are tons of examples.

Ezekiel means strong God
Gabriel means strength of God
Elijah means God is Jehovah
Isaiah means salvation from Jehovah.
Peniel means face of God
Othniel means force of God
Israel means to struggle against God

These names are rather interesting. As in the case of Ishmael (pbuh), they are used as actions or attributes of God, but most certainly not the entire personification of that action or attribute or the personification of God. Examples like Gabriel or strength of God may be used to show God's strength using an angel, but he as the angel is not the totality of God's strength, only a vessel by which some of the strength is demonstrated. If Gabriel is the total strength of God, then he is a part of God. The same is true for Othniel as a faculty which God used to display his Force, but he is not God's total force. This is quite similar to the declaration that God is the only savior, despite the Bible's documentation of numerous human saviors. Perhaps something to ponder is the meaning of Isaiah as "salvation from Jehovah" and the meaning of Jesus' (pbuh) name in Hebrew is "Jehovah is salvation." Both names denote salvation, but it is Jesus (pbuh) who is exalted as the only Savior. Why is that?

All this considered, it is a mistake of Trinitarians to conclude that the name, Immanuel, literally means that Jesus (pbuh) was God with them. More correctly, it means God is using Jesus (pbuh) to be with them just as he used every prophet. Actually the claim that this prophecy is in reference to Jesus (pbuh) is another problem in itself.

Jews do not take this passage as a prophecy of the coming Messiah, but a promise fulfilled long before Jesus (pbuh) was born. The passage is in reference to King Ahaz and his people to assure them that God is with them in their rivalry with two other kingdoms. And the proof or sign that God is with them will be a child born named Immanuel of a young woman. The term "virgin" in Isaiah 7:14 is a mistranslation of the word, "almah" meaning young woman. "Bethulah" is the Hebrew word for virgin.

Many speculate that this mistranslations is intentional and a blatant attempt to insert Jesus (pbuh) into the role of "God with us," even though Immanuel is a name, not a role. Even more surprising is the fact that Jesus (pbuh) is never called Immanuel by anyone as the prophecy claims. Matthew's gospel reiterates that they shall call Jesus' (pbuh) name Immanuel. But no one called him this in his lifetime. On the contrary,

Luke 1:30 *And the angel said unto her, Fear not, Mary: for thou hast found favour with God.*
Luke 1:31 *And, behold, thou shalt conceive in thy womb, and bring forth a son, and shalt call his name JESUS.*

In fact, Acts 10:38 states that God was with Jesus (pbuh). It is impossible to be with someone and be that someone simultaneously. For instance the disciple, Matthew was with Jesus (pbuh), but he was not Jesus (pbuh). But through the gospel of Matthew, Jesus (pbuh) is with us. In like manner, God is with us through the works of Jesus (pbuh), though he is not God. This same message is conveyed in the story of the rich man, Lazarus and Abraham (pbuh) (Luke 16:20-31).

The rich man was in agony in hell and Lazarus was in heaven and the rich man asked Abraham (pbuh) to send Lazarus to warn his brothers of the torments of hell, that they may repent their sins. Abraham (pbuh) answered that "They have Moses (pbuh) and the prophets, let them hear them." Moses (pbuh) and the prophets were not on Earth to guide man, but their teachings and works were with the people to guide them, therefore Abraham declares that Moses (pbut) and the prophets were with the people. The logical explanation of the name Immanuel, whether it pertains to Jesus (pbuh) or whomever, is that God is with us through his message which he gave to his prophets, not that God will actually come to earth.

Another thing to consider is that Jesus (pbuh), on the cross, asks God, why he forsook him (Matt. 27:46). If we are to believe that Jesus (pbuh) was not lying, then at that moment God was not with him. So how could Jesus (pbuh) be God with us?

THE MIGHTY GOD

Isaiah 9:6 *"and his name shall be called Wonderful, Counselor, The mighty God, The everlasting Father, The Prince of Peace."*

Just as Hebrew scholars and the Jewish people take exception to Immanuel being identified with Jesus (pbuh), they also take exception to this verse as a description of Jesus (pbuh). They say this verse had already been fulfilled before Jesus (pbuh) was born. The translation "wonderful, counselor" and the insertion of several commas are also in dispute. But because, none of these issues are pertinent to or a detriment to the case against Jesus' (pbuh) divinity, they will be overlooked for this books purpose. I have no problem with the idea that Jesus (pbuh) was wonderful and a counselor, but there may be some issues as it pertains to "The mighty God," "The everlasting Father" and "The Prince of Peace."

As was written earlier, Jesus (pbuh) is not qualified to be called "the Prince of Peace" considering the fact that he admitted that he did not come for peace on two different occasions. Even further, someone who would require his followers to hate their mothers and fathers and children, his siblings and even himself (Luke 14:26), must not be confused with someone on a peaceful mission. All this is significant because Jesus (pbuh) says the peacemakers are sons of God. Thus he is not to be confused with the person here described as the Prince of Peace and there is a case here to exclude him from even being the "son of God" literally and metaphorically. Perhaps the most troubling name or title here is "the everlasting Father." This title goes against the Trinity, against Jesus' (pbuh) words and against common sense and comprehension, because Jesus (pbuh) is the Son, not the Father.

The creed explicitly states:
24. So there is one Father, not three Fathers; one Son, not three Sons; one Holy Spirit, not three Holy Spirits.

Jesus (pbuh) says you must pray "our Father," not "our fathers" (Matt. 6:9) and Jesus (pbuh) said "my father and your father" (John 20:17). Some Christians may say that Jesus (pbuh) is the Son of God, but the Father of man, then the name should have been "Your everlasting Father" not "The everlasting Father." There is no biblical scripture substantiating the idea that Jesus (pbuh) is our Father. On the contrary, Jesus (pbuh) says call no man on earth "father," because your father IS IN HEAVEN (Matt. 23:9). Therefore the term "father" is not pertaining to Jesus (pbuh).

What about "mighty God"? Like the case of Immanuel, no one ever called his name "mighty God." This is where names like Ezekiel means "strong God" and Elijah means "God is Jehovah" come into play. Even if someone had called Jesus (pbuh), "mighty God," there is no indication that this is to be taken literally. If it is to be taken literally, then Ezekiel and Elijah must be re-evaluated. Also, the Bible has set a precedent where others who are not God Almighty can be called god, but the translators use their capitals and lower cases to "help" the reader understand.

Psalms 82:6 *"I have said, Ye are gods; and all of you are children of the most High."*

In this verse God himself addresses these men as gods. God also called Moses (pbuh) a god to pharaoh (Exodus 7:1). 2Corinthians 4:4 describes the devil as god of this world. Samuel was described as a god (1Sam. 28:13-14). This conclusively shows that the term "god" in the Bible is not to be identified with the Supreme Being whenever it occurs. All these beings are mighty, but none of them are Almighty.

Since Jesus (pbuh) is not the "Prince of Peace" or "the everlasting Father" and "the mighty God" is ambiguous, we are forced to reconsider who was the prophecy for? Jews do not believe this to be a prophecy of the Messiah, which they still await, but a description of someone already born before these words were written by Isaiah. They consider Hezekiah as the fulfillment of this verse and they deem the usage of the present tense in these verses to be incorrect. They assert that the beginning of Isaiah 9:6 in Hebrew, "yeled yalad ben nathan misrah shekem," should read

"For a child has been born to us, a son has been given us. And authority has settled on his shoulders," whereas the KJV translates it as, "For unto us a child is born, unto us a son is given: and the government shall be upon his shoulder."

Whether this passage is a prophecy of Jesus (pbuh) is questionable, but even if it is about Jesus (pbuh), this is insufficient evidence to prove his divinity, because these titles are either given to people other than Jesus (pbuh) or they conflict with the nature or words of Jesus (pbuh).

JESUS (PBUH) WORSHIPPED

In Exodus 20:5, 23:24, and 34:14, God in no uncertain terms says that he is a jealous God that commands his people to bow down and worship no other God before him. He even warns of the punishment for such an infraction. For this sin, the Bible says that God will "visit the iniquity of the father upon his children and their children up to the fourth generation." In other words, this is a major sin in God's eyes. Moses and Aaron (pbut) (Num. 16:20-22), Abraham (pbuh) (Gen. 24:52), Ezekiel (pbuh) (Ez. 9:8), the disciples (Matt. 17:6), all of Judah and the inhabitants of Jerusalem (2Chr 20:18) and even Jesus (pbuh) (Matt. 26:39) fell on their faces and worshipped God. When Jesus (pbuh) prayed to God, the idea that he is God is put in jeopardy, unless you consider that he is a lesser God than God Almighty. The alternatives are that Jesus (pbuh) was only gesturing and he knew he was God, or he did not know that he was God. If he was gesturing, then he was deceiving his disciples, which can't be accepted from God or a man of God. If he did not know that he was God, then he was not God in the first place, because God is all-knowing. Nevertheless, the Bible documents numerous people bowing down to others beside God. The question is whether they were worshipping these other people besides God.

Abigail bowed down to David (pbuh) (1Sam. 25:23-24), a Shunammite woman bowed to Elisha (pbuh) (2Kings 4:37) and Moses (pbuh) bowed down to his father-in-law, Jethro (Ex.18:7). The King Nebuchadnezzar bowed down and worshipped Daniel (Dan. 2:46), as well. Are these people being worshipped as God? Probably not. It seems that worship has several connotations and it is used in different forms in the Bible. Elisha raised this woman's son from the dead and "she fell to his feet and bowed herself to the ground." This would seem to be in direct contradiction to the commandment given by God not to bow down to and serve another God. But we must not forget that the Bible says "God is the only savior" and even though others are authorized to use the title "savior" because they are agents of God. It is not a stretch to understand that this women is worshipping God when she is bowing down before God's agent, Elisha (pbuh). And Abigail, Moses (pbuh) and

Nebauchadnezzar were making similar gestures or gestures of respect.

It has been boldly stated that Jesus (pbuh) never unambiguously declared divinity and he never commanded others to worship him. It becomes apparent to Trinitarians that this is indeed true, so they are forced to come up with another angle to justify their position. In response to this reality, they present the support for Jesus' (pbuh) divinity as citations of people worshipping Jesus (pbuh) (Matt. 2:2, 2:8, 14:33, John 9:38) and Jesus (pbuh) did not condemn these actions. They argue that because Jesus (pbuh) did not condemn their worship of Him, then he must have accepted their worship because he is God. Just as in other instances, a particular word or phrase is used in the Bible and it is not understood literally or in its most strict form, unless it is in reference to Jesus (pbuh). The words "worship" or "bow down" can be understood to mean adoration or paying homage to a person as an agent of God and not God himself. But let's explore the claim that the absence of reproof is evidence of divinity.

The Trinitarian maintains that if Jesus (pbuh) did not correct an act then he acknowledges its legitimacy. Considering the facts that nothing of Jesus' (pbuh) life is recorded with great authority in the gospels, there are stories about his life which differ from gospel to gospel and his words and deeds are extremely condensed into these short narratives. It is without doubt absent a great number of details about this man, Jesus (pbuh). To place your faith in the Trinity based upon absence of reproof is perhaps unreasonable. Jesus (pbuh) was called a winebibber and a gluttonous person (Luke 7:34) and he did not deny this.

According to the reasoning used by Trinitarians, it is therefore very likely that he was a winebibber and gluttonous. Is anyone willing to concede this? Probably not. David (pbuh), Jethro, Daniel and Elisha (pbuh) had someone bow before them, yet none of them reprimanded those bowing down to them. Should we consider that these four people are implying that they are God? No, it can't even be said that they inferred divinity to themselves, because this implies that they spoke on the matter. But they were completely silent, as Jesus (pbuh) was according to the Bible. If someone calls another person an idiot and this person doesn't respond, is this conclusive evidence that he/she is an idiot? Not at all. Thus it is not wise to exalt someone to the highest position imaginable with similar reasoning. Jesus (pbuh) does speak about God and his worship on a different occasion. First he instructs his followers to pray to the Father, not to himself. More importantly he says

John 4:23 *But the hour cometh, and now is, when the true worshippers shall worship the Father in spirit and in truth: for the Father seeketh such to worship him.*
John 4:24 *God [is] a Spirit: and they that worship him must worship [him] in spirit and in truth.*

This is actually the correction of the people worshipping Jesus (pbuh). The Bible did not record Jesus (pbuh) speaking against people worshipping him on other occasions, but on this specific occasion, Jesus (pbuh) seems to be correcting some people's practices, when he describes a TRUE worshipper. He says, a true worshipper worships the Father, thus a false worshipper worships anyone or anything else. So the worship of the Son is not a practice of a true worshipper. This would render all the worship of Jesus (pbuh) incorrect. Also notice that Jesus (pbuh) is using God and the Father synonymously, though he never uses "the Son" or the "Holy Spirit" synonymously with God. And with all this talk of God and the Father, spirit and worship, this is a golden opportunity for Jesus (pbuh) to say "I am God" or "worship me," yet he feels obliged to only confess that he is the Christ (John 4:25).

We find in the story of Jesus (pbuh) being tempted by the devil, that the devil offers Jesus (pbuh) an amazing proposition. He takes Jesus (pbuh) to a high mountain and shows him all the kingdoms of the world and offers Jesus dominion over all of it, if Jesus worships him (Luke 4:5-8). This story is amazing on many different levels, two of them being the idea that the devil offered "God" dominion over the world and he asked "God" to worship him. Did he not know that Jesus (pbuh) was God and ruler of the entire universe? And why didn't Jesus (pbuh) "correct" this tremendous blunder? What was he implying, by not saying to the devil, "You fool, how can you offer me what is already mines?"

What does Jesus' (pbuh) silence on this matter indicate? Maybe that he does not have dominion over the world. Or maybe he felt it more pertinent to comment on the idea of worship. So Jesus (pbuh) says worship God and serve him. Jesus' (pbuh) response implied to the devil and the reader that Jesus (pbuh) worshipped God, which has been documented in the gospels (Matt. 26:39, Luke 22:41-42). With either option, it becomes apparent that people worshipping Jesus (pbuh) is insufficient evidence to declare his divinity, when he himself worships someone else.

Revelations 22:8 is often cited to substantiate the claim that Jesus' (pbuh) silence indicates his divinity, because an angel doesn't accept worship from John. The angel tells him to worship God, just as Jesus (pbuh) said. In light of the fact that every person mentioned as being worshipped made no such gesture of deterrence, it may be understood that angels are not privileged to certain things given to a man of god or that the word "worship" was used as praying, instead of paying homage.

In any case, the angel tells John to worship God, not the Son or Jesus (pbuh). If angels and more importantly Jesus (pbuh) instructs his followers to worship God the Father, how does it come to pass that Christians pray to and worship Jesus (pbuh)? This practice is not to be attributed to the religion from Jesus (pbuh) or the religion of Jesus (pbuh), but it is attributed to those who misinterpreted his words and shaped the doctrine about him according to their misunderstanding.

JESUS (PBUH) FORGAVE SINS

It has been said that since Jesus (pbuh) forgave people's sin that he is God, because only God can forgive sins. This claim is probably not from Catholics, who happen to be the largest group of Christians on earth. Catholics have a well known custom of confessing one's sins to the clergyman and the clergyman declares that their sins are forgiven. Yet he is not considered to be a god, but a spokesmen for god. Is this the role which Jesus (pbuh) holds? The story of a cripple man Jesus (pbuh) healed is a good example to examine how and why Jesus (pbuh) forgave sin.

Luke 5:18 *And, behold, men brought in a bed a man which was taken with a palsy: and they sought [means] to bring him in, and to lay [him] before him.*
Luke 5:19 *And when they could not find by what [way] they might bring him in because of the multitude, they went upon the housetop, and let him down through the tiling with [his] couch into the midst before Jesus.*
Luke 5:20 *And when he saw their faith, he said unto him, Man, thy sins are forgiven thee.*
Luke 5:21 *And the scribes and the Pharisees began to reason, saying, Who is this which speaketh blasphemies? Who can forgive sins, but God alone?*
Luke 5:22 *But when Jesus perceived their thoughts, he answering said unto them, What reason ye in your hearts?*
Luke 5:23 *Whether is easier, to say, Thy sins be forgiven thee; or to say, Rise up and walk?*
Luke 5:24 *But that ye may know that the Son of man hath power upon earth to forgive sins, (he said unto the sick of the palsy,) I say unto thee, Arise, and take up thy couch, and go into thine house.*
Luke 5:25 *And immediately he rose up before them, and took that up whereon he lay, and departed to his own house, glorifying God.*
Luke 5:26 *And they were all amazed, and they glorified God, and were filled with fear, saying, We have seen strange things today.*

The first point of peculiarity is that this story is in all three synoptic gospels Matthew, Mark, and Luke, but the gospel of John has a different setting and a different dispute between Jesus (pbuh) and the scribes and Pharisees. The synoptic gospels have the story taking place in Capernaum, while John writes of the story in Jerusalem and the Jews condemned Jesus (pbuh) for healing on the Sabbath, not for forgiving sins. The second point is that Jesus (pbuh) says the SON OF MAN has power to forgive sins. The Son of Man is the human nature of Jesus (pbuh), not his divinity. Therefore the question is, "how can a man forgive another's sins?" The third point is that Jesus (pbuh) forgave his sins because of the faith of the people that brought him to Jesus (pbuh), not for anything that the man did. This in itself is quite strange, because it makes no mention of the man seeking forgiveness and Jesus (pbuh) does not forgive the sins of those who brought him. But for argument sake, let's suppose that Jesus (pbuh) did forgive the man's sins. Does this make him God?

On face value, this may be an implication of divinity, if it is placed in solidarity. But if one simply considers other sayings of Jesus (pbuh), the answer becomes clear. Jesus (pbuh) says he can do NOTHING of himself (John 5:19) and the Father GIVES him the authority to judge (John 5:22). God is void of nothing, especially power and authority. No one can give God anything. These words of Jesus (pbuh) about his ability to judge, cripples the argument for his divinity. The logical reconciliation between the story of Jesus' (pbuh) forgiveness and the fact that he can do nothing without God is that God forgave the man through Jesus (pbuh), just as he healed the man through Jesus (pbuh). And the people who saw this miracle "glorified God," not Jesus (pbuh). Matthew 9:8 explains further that the people glorified God because he had "given such authority to human beings."

To further illustrate this point, consider that Jesus (pbuh) says that "all power is GIVEN unto me" (Matt. 28:18) and that his words are not actually his but those of the Father (John 12:49). Therefore the Father actually forgave the man's sin, not Jesus (pbuh). And though Jesus (pbuh) is given authority to judge, he too delegates the authority to his disciple, who will judge the 12 tribes of Israel (Luke 22:30). In this judgment, it is obvious that the disciples will pardon some and punish others, yet this authority does not give them equality with God. Why does a double standard apply to Jesus (pbuh)?

Something to ponder is that on Jesus' (pbuh) critical and most vulnerable hour, he did not say "I forgive you, my enemies." On the contrary Jesus (pbuh) said, "Forgive them, Father! They don't know what they are doing." (Luke 23:34) It is apparent who the ultimate authority of forgiveness belongs to.

LORD OF THE SABBATH

__Mark 2:23__ And it came to pass, that he went through the corn fields on the Sabbath day; and his disciples began, as they went, to pluck the ears of corn.
__Mark 2:24__ And the Pharisees said unto him, Behold, why do they on the Sabbath day that which is not lawful?
__Mark 2:25__ And he said unto them, Have ye never read what David did, when he had need, and was an hungred, he, and they that were with him?
__Mark 2:26__ How he went into the house of God in the days of Abiathar the high priest, and did eat the shewbread, which is not lawful to eat but for the priests, and gave also to them which were with him?
__Mark 2:27__ And he said unto them, The Sabbath was made for man, and not man for the Sabbath:
__Mark 2:28__ Therefore the Son of man is Lord also of the Sabbath

This story is used to say that Jesus (pbuh) is God because he is able to break the law of the Sabbath. This interpretation has been used and supported by evangelist, who would like to pull verse 28 apart from the rest of the story. This story may also be told from Luke 6:1-11, which omits the words of Jesus (pbuh) in Mark 2:27. Yet this verse is a very crucial part of this story. The version of the story in Matthew 12:3-8 includes these words:

Matthew 12:5 *Or have ye not read in the law, how that on the Sabbath days the priests in the temple profane the Sabbath, and are blameless?*
Matthew 12:6 *But I say unto you, That in this place is [one] greater than the temple.*
Matthew 12:7 *But if ye had known what [this] meaneth, I will have mercy, and not sacrifice, ye would not have condemned the guiltless.*

But it also omits the verse found in Mark 2:27. In consistency
with its reputation, the gospel of John mentions an entirely different episode, but it has the same premise.

John 7:21 *Jesus answered and said to them, "I performed one work and all of you are amazed*
John 7:22 *because of it. Moses gave you circumcision--not that it came from Moses but rather from the patriarchs--and you circumcise a man on the Sabbath.*
John 7:23 *If a man can receive circumcision on a Sabbath so that the law of Moses may not be broken, are you angry with me because I made a whole person well on a Sabbath?*
John 7:24 *Stop judging by appearances, but judge justly."*

First we must explain that the Sabbath is said to be the day in which is understood by Jews to be Saturday, no work of any kind is permitted. Because God rested on this day, it is prescribed for all Jews to rest, as well. Now on a Sabbath day, we found, only from Matthew, why Jesus (pbuh) and the disciples violated this law. Matthew says that they were hungry so they plucked some ears of corn to eat. The Pharisees, perhaps waiting for Jesus (pbuh) to make a mistake, asked why Jesus (pbuh) is breaking the Sabbath. To this Jesus (pbuh) replied that David (pbuh) broke the Sabbath out of necessity and certain priest justifiably profaned the temple on the Sabbath day. This is to say, that one must consider the circumstances before placing judgment on another. Jesus (pbuh) cleverly uses those whom the Jews held in high esteem to convey this message. To bring this point home Jesus (pbuh) says "The Sabbath was made for man, and not man for the Sabbath." This verse is very important in this context, because it sets the stage for the following verse.

In the next verse Jesus (pbuh) says " THEREFORE the Son of man is Lord also of the Sabbath." The word "therefore" at the beginning of verse 28 of Mark informs the reader that it is a result of or a continuation of the former verse. The title "son of man" again is personifying and magnifying the humanity of Jesus (pbuh). Thus he is stating that he is lord and master of the Sabbath just as every person is when it comes to necessity. In some instances it is permissible to break the law of the Sabbath. This is why he says the Sabbath is made for man, meaning for his benefit and well-being. If it causes man undue hardship, then it is contrary to his well-being, thus contradicts its own purpose.

In Matthew 12:11-12, Jesus (pbuh) makes things even more practical. He asked "if a man's sheep fell in a pit on the Sabbath, wouldn't he get it out?" Jesus (pbuh) is applying "common sense" and reasoning to the law, to show that there is an exception to every rule. However, if one reads Matthew and Luke without Mark, it gives a false indication that Jesus (pbuh) simply transgressed the laws because he is the Lord of the Sabbath. Actually the totality of Jesus' (pbuh) words gives every man authority over the Sabbath in this manner, thus making them lord of the Sabbath as David (pbuh) and the priest were. And remember that Jesus (pbuh) too was GIVEN authority (Matt. 28:18). He didn't already have authority. He had to acquire it from God.

MIRACLES

The miracles of Jesus (pbuh) are sometimes construed as evidence for his divinity. But are miracles understood in the Bible to prove that the person performing the acts is God or is that person just a representative of God? Turning water into blood, causing famine in Egypt and parting the Red Sea are all miracles used by Moses (pbuh) as a representative of God. Miracles can be performed in the name of demons (Matt. 12:27), and false Christs and false prophets can perform miracles (Matt. 24:24). People can even perform miracles and cast out devils in Jesus' (pbuh) name, though Jesus (pbuh) will rebuke them (Matt. 7:22). John 5:2-4 mentions a body of water in which the afflicted enter and were healed. Though it seems miracles occurred frequently in the Bible, they are not always a sign of being true, or being righteous, let alone being God. If miracles make you God, those who believe in the Bible must be polytheist.

Jesus (pbuh) performed many miracles and they were extraordinary, but his miracles require a prerequisite, faith. On several occasions Jesus (pbuh) claims that the people's faith was the reason for the miracle's occurrence (Mark 5:36, Mark 9:23, 10:51 5:34). Therefore it is reasonable to believe that his miracles were hampered or stagnated from a lack of faith. In one instance, Jesus (pbuh) was unsuccessful in his first effort to completely restore a blind man's sight. However on his second effort, Jesus (pbuh) did restore the man's sight (Mark 8:22-26). This suggests that he needed to conjure up more power or that the man's faith had to be strengthened in order to accomplish this feat. Confirmation of the later hypothesis is found in Mark 6:5.

<u>Mark 6:5</u> *He could do no mighty work there, except that he laid his hands on a few sick people, and healed them. He marveled because of their unbelief.*

On another occasion, Jesus (pbuh) sent the disciples out to heal an ill man. Their efforts were ineffective, due to the disciple's unbelief. Jesus (pbuh) told them nothing would be impossible to them, if they have just a little faith (Matt. 17:14-20). In Mark 5:30-32, one woman's faith was so strong that by simply touching Jesus' (pbuh) clothing, an ailment she had for 12 years was cured. We are told in this story that Jesus (pbuh) did not know who had touched his garment and taken some of "his power." There is a point to be made here. It is apparent that Jesus' (pbuh) miracles are not his own possession, but something given to him for usage under qualifying circumstances. The specifications were that the person administering the miracle and the person given the miracle must have faith. This raises the question, in whom did Jesus (pbuh) place his faith? If Jesus (pbuh) is God, why is his miracles limited and why is his power is limited? When the woman was cured, he did not know who touched him, so it's clear that he did not administer the cure, yet the woman was healed. Jesus' (pbuh) miraculous powers were obviously not under his control, but he was given his power (Matt. 28:18) abundantly to give to the faithful, by the one in whom he placed his faith.

The great miracles of Jesus (pbuh) have no exclusivity to him. Just as Jesus (pbuh) did, Elisha (pbuh) feed multitudes with a small amount of bread (2Kings 4:42-44), he healed the lepers (2Kings 5:10-14), and cured blindness (2Kings 6:15-24). Though some miracles performed by Jesus (pbuh) are not recorded as being done by Elisha (pbuh) or the prophet Elijah (pbuh), another miracle worker, it is not a stretch of the imagination to believe that the Bible does not record every miracle performed by these two individuals. They do not have biographies dedicated to the documentation of their lives as the four gospels are for Jesus (pbuh). These four gospels don't even contain every miracle of Jesus (pbuh). This is evident in the story of Jesus (pbuh) turning water into wine. Jesus' (pbuh) mother, upon seeing the wine shortage at a wedding, asked Jesus (pbuh) to help the people with their problem. Obviously, she had prior knowledge that Jesus (pbuh) could perform miracles, yet the source for her confidence in Jesus' (pbuh) powers is not documented in the gospels.

Martha, the sister of Lazarus, had confidence that Jesus (pbuh) could perform miracles with God's help (John 11:21-22). And John confirms that "many other signs truly did Jesus in the presence of his disciples, which are not written in this book" (John 20:30-31). So if many of Jesus (pbuh) miracles are absent in his four biographies, then it is obvious that many miracles performed by other prophets of God were not recorded.

Also, there are miracles performed by the Elisha and Elijah which would be presumably useful to Jesus (pbut) in his times of persecution and even in his times of hunger (Mark 11:12). Elijah (pbuh) caused the rain to cease for 3 1/2 years (1Kings 17:1, 2), he also caused it to rain (1Kings 18:45,) he was fed by the ravens (1Kings 17:4), he called fire from heaven on the altar (1Kings 18:37-38), he parted the Jordan River (2Kings 2:8), and he was taken up to heaven in a whirlwind (2Kings 2:10-12). Elisha (pbuh) parted the Jordan River (2Kings 2:14), he healed the waters (2Kings 2:21), he filled the entire valley with water (2Kings 3:17) and he resurrected a man touched by his dead bones (2Kings 13:21). While Jesus (pbuh) cursed a tree and caused it to die, Aaron's (pbuh) rod, an inanimate object, became a snake, by God's permission (Ex. 7:10-12). That fact that the giving of life is done by God is clearly expressed in this story. In the same manner, Joseph (pbuh) interpreted dreams. Time and time again, when Joseph (pbuh) was asked to interpret a dream, when he did, he never accepted the credit. He gave all the credit to God (Gen. 40:8, 41:16).

Both Elisha and Elijah, returned someone to life as Jesus (pbut) did. And a commonality between these stories and Aaron's story is the credit for the miracle of life is given to God by these righteous men (1Kings 17:20-23, 2Kings 4:30-36). All three of these men invoke the supreme source of power to give life to someone or something. So what about Jesus (pbuh)?

Jesus (pbuh) is credited with the resurrection of a man named Lazarus. Two women, Martha and Mary, had a brother named Lazarus, who was very ill. They were friends of Jesus (pbuh), so they knew of his miraculous powers. They sent word to him that Lazarus was sick and they needed Jesus' (pbuh) help. Jesus (pbuh) waited 2 days before traveling to see Lazarus, but by that time Lazarus had died. Jesus (pbuh) went to visit them anyway. Martha, upon hearing of Jesus' (pbuh) trip, met him outside of town, and her sister, Mary and the Jews followed behind her.

John 11:33 *When Jesus therefore saw her weeping, and the Jews also weeping which came with her, he groaned in the spirit, and was troubled,*
John 11:34 *And said, Where have ye laid him? They said unto him, Lord, come and see.*
John 11:35 *Jesus wept.*
John 11:36 *Then said the Jews, Behold how he loved him!*
John 11:37 *And some of them said, Could not this man, which opened the eyes of the blind, have caused that even this man should not have died?*
John 11:38 *Jesus therefore again groaning in himself cometh to the grave. It was a cave, and a stone lay upon it.*
John 11:39 *Jesus said, Take ye away the stone. Martha, the sister of him that was dead, saith unto him, Lord, by this time he stinketh: for he hath been [dead] four days.*
John 11:40 *Jesus saith unto her, Said I not unto thee, that, if thou wouldest believe, thou shouldest see the glory of God?*
John 11:41 *Then they took away the stone [from the place] where the dead was laid. And Jesus lifted up [his] eyes, and said, Father, I thank thee that thou hast heard me.*

John 11:42 *And I knew that thou hearest me always: but because of the people which stand by I said [it], that they may believe that thou hast sent me.*
John 11:43 *And when he thus had spoken, he cried with a loud voice, Lazarus, come forth.*
John 11:44 *And he that was dead came forth, bound hand and foot with graveclothes: and his face was bound about with a napkin. Jesus saith unto them, Loose him, and let him go.*
John 11:45 *Then many of the Jews which came to Mary, and had seen the things which Jesus did, believed on him*

If you notice, throughout the story Jesus (pbuh) is harping on the belief of the sisters and his disciples. This is again the criteria for his miraculous powers to work. But what is of greater importance is the groaning of Jesus (pbuh). At first glances, it appears to be groaning in sorrow and sadness due to the sight of Mary and the Jews crying. But it says that Jesus (pbuh) "groaned in the spirit" and then he groaned again "in himself" as he was approaching the grave. As they opened the cave, Jesus (pbuh) becomes more brazen and begins speaking audibly. He declares that they will see the glory of God, just as he insisted earlier. Then it becomes apparent what Jesus (pbuh) was doing when he was "groaning in the spirit" and "groaning in himself."

He was praying to God to help him bring Lazarus back to life. This is clear when we read that Jesus (pbuh) lifts up his eyes and thanks God for hearing him. This would explain why Jesus began talking so boldly. Perhaps God gave him an indication that his prayers were answered. Jesus (pbuh) continues that God always hears him, but he was speaking this way because of the people that stood by. Jesus (pbuh) wanted them to understand that he was sent by God. He was trying to make sure the people wouldn't mistakenly conclude that he performed this miracle. It was the work of the one who sent him, God. He was giving credit to God just as the other prophets of God did, when they performed a miracle. Jesus (pbuh) knew that people would be susceptible to calling him God and in his lifetime, he made an effort to stop this problem at its inception. And Jesus (pbuh) was successful in his efforts because the people gave the credit to the deserving party.

Matthew 9:8 *But when the multitudes saw [it], they marvelled, and glorified God, which had given such power unto men.*

The multitudes understand what Jesus (pbuh) was trying to convey, that he was a prophet, a messenger, an agent and a representative of God, but he was not God. And he is not alone in presenting this message. Luke echoes this very sentiment in the book of Acts.

Acts 2:22 *Ye men of Israel, hear these words; Jesus of Nazareth, a man approved of God among you by miracles and wonders and signs, WHICH GOD DID BY HIM in the midst of you, as ye yourselves also know*

THE RESURRECTION

One awesome miracle of Jesus (pbuh) in the Bible not yet mentioned is his resurrection. However, there are several reasons for doubting its authenticity. One being that the story of the resurrection of Jesus (pbuh) at the end of Mark is consider by Bible scholars to be an interpolation. The oldest copies of the gospels do not contain this rendition of the resurrection and most translations have a commentary section at the end of Mark's gospel, which testifies to this fact. Mark's gospel ends abruptly, with Mary looking into Jesus' (pbuh) sepulcher in 16:8. And to compound matters, later manuscripts of Mark, which contain the resurrection, have variant readings. So the translators must decide which version of the resurrection they will use. And considering that Mark is the oldest gospel and the source from which Luke and Matthew are derived, the story of the resurrection has some authenticity problems. Something else to consider is that Paul, not the authors of the Gospels, was the first to teach this doctrine. The letter to the Corinthians is considered to be the 1st writings on the Resurrection contained in the Bible. Which means Mark, who was not an eyewitness to the events surrounding Jesus (pbuh) and the alleged resurrection, probably got his information from Paul, who did not witness the event either.

Another problems is the fact that the witnesses to the supposed crucifixion and at least two angels said that Jesus (pbuh) was ALIVE (Mark 16:11, Luke 24:5, 23), not RESURRECTED. If someone asserts that a person presumed to be dead is RESURRECTED, they mean that the person did die, but he is now raised back to life. But if someone says that the same person is ALIVE, they are declaring that he was mistakenly thought to be dead.

Also, we must consider the fact that after his alleged crucifixion, Jesus (pbuh) ate food and he had a physical body (Luke 24:36-43), when he is supposed to be a resurrected spiritual being. Acts 1:13 explicitly states that Jesus (pbuh) gave many convincing proofs that he was ALIVE. A resurrected person has an immortal and spiritual body as stated by Paul and Jesus (pbuh) (1Cor. 15:44, Luke

24:39-43, Luke 20:35-36). So it would appear that at least two of those convincing proofs that he was ALIVE was the eating of the broiled fish and honey comb and his disciples witnessing his physical body.

We must remember that after the devil tempted Jesus (pbuh), an angel ministered to him (Matthew 4:11). And when Jesus (pbuh) was praying with sweat like drops of blood to be saved from the cross, an angel strengthened him (Luke 22:43-44). It is clear that this angel comes to revitalize Jesus (pbuh) and replenish any of his deficiency in his times of need. Some Christians say the angel strengthens his spirit to accept his demise, but the book of Hebrews gives another answer.

Hebrews 5:7 *Who in the days of his flesh, when he had offered up prayers and supplications with strong crying and tears unto him that was able to save him from death, and was heard in that he feared*

After Jesus (pbuh) asks God to save him, we see that God sent this angel to strengthen Jesus (pbuh). Why would you need strength to die or to accept death, when the gospels are littered with Jesus (pbuh) predicting his own death? One is granted strength in order to sustain this energy and health to stay alive. And Hebrews 5 say that Jesus (pbuh) asked to be SAVED from death by HIM THAT WAS ABLE TO SAVE HIM. It seems that Jesus (pbuh) didn't want to be the sacrifice for the world and that he could not save himself. What is truly amazing is that the Bible says Jesus' (pbuh) prayers were HEARD. When Ishmael (pbuh) was given his name it was because God heard Abraham's (pbuh) prayers. We find that a heard prayer to God is an answered prayer in

Biblical terms. The name, Ishmael (pbuh), as previously mentioned literally means God hears (prayers).

Therefore when Jesus (pbuh) prayed to be saved from death (Matt. 26:39), the book of Hebrews informs us that God did hear and answer his prayer by sending his angel to save him from death. The following words of Jesus (pbuh) and James confirm my stance.

John 11:42 *And I (Jesus) knew that thou (God) hearest me always*

James 5:16 *The prayer of a righteous man is powerful and effective.*

The final point to be made on this subject is with Jesus' (pbuh) promised miracle to the Jews. He says he will be in the belly of the earth AS JONAH (pbuh) WAS in the belly of the whale for three days and three nights (Matt 12:38-40). Well, Jonah (pbuh) was ALIVE before he went into the whale, he was ALIVE when he was inside of the whale and he was ALIVE when he came out of the whale. Yet Christians swear that Jesus (pbuh) was DEAD when he went into the earth, DEAD inside of the earth and RESURRECTED when he came out. This is quite UNLIKE Jonah (pbuh). Like Daniel's salvation from the lion (Dan. 6:1828), Jonah (pbuh) was saved from the fish (Jonah 2:1-10). And in order for Jesus to be like Jonah (pbut), he must have been saved from his demise. The miracle of Jonah (pbuh) was his survival in a situation in which he was by all means supposed to die. When Jesus (pbuh) promises the same miracle, we are forced to ask ourselves, did he fulfill his promise?

I must admit that there exists clear statements that Jesus (pbuh) was killed in the Bible, yet in the accounts of the crucifixion, there is more than enough evidence to believe otherwise. The proclamation of Jesus' (pbuh) crucifixion by some, does not negate the existence of proof to the contrary. As we have seen with the primary topic being dealt with in this book, just because a multitude of people believe and declare a thing with conviction, does not make it so. [For further proof that Jesus (pbuh) was not crucified, read "Jesus (pbuh) Was Not Crucified"]

GREATER THAN THE TEMPLE

Matthew 12:3 He answered, "Haven't you read what David did when he and his companions were hungry?
Matthew 12:4 He entered the house of God, and he and his companions ate the consecrated bread—which was not lawful for them to do, but only for the priests.
Matthew 12:5 Or haven't you read in the Law that on the Sabbath the priests in the temple desecrate the day and yet are innocent?
Matthew 12:6 I tell you that one greater than the temple is here.
Matthew 12:7 If you had known what these words mean, 'I desire mercy, not sacrifice', you would not have condemned the innocent.
Matthew 12:8 For the Son of Man is Lord of the Sabbath."

Some people suggest that Jesus (pbuh) is making reference to his divinity in this instance. Though verse 6 has been translated as "one, someone or something is greater than the temple is here" and Jesus (pbuh) does not specify who this person or thing is, let us assume that he is speaking of himself. The Temple of Solomon is of great significance to the Jews, but Jesus (pbuh) says he is greater than the temple. From this statement we can conclude nothing further, especially when Jesus (pbuh) is reported to have said that "the Father is greater than I." These two statements place him somewhere higher than the temple but lower than the Father and God is lower than no one. These verses fall in perfect alignment with my claim that Jesus (pbuh) is but a messenger of God.

THE SEVEN I AM'S

All of the "I am" declarations supposedly made by Jesus (pbuh) were only recorded by John. Often Trinitarians use these phrases to postulate the point that Jesus (pbuh) was placing divinity upon himself. If they are read collectively, and without reference to the context in which Jesus (pbuh) was speaking, it might appear that Jesus (pbuh) is giving himself divine attributes, but let's have a look at the phrases separately and in their proper context.

"I am the Light of the World"

<u>John 8:12</u> *Then spake Jesus again unto them, saying, I am the light of the world: he that followeth me shall not walk in darkness, but shall have the light of life.*

If one only states the words "I am the light of the world," it is apparent how this can be understood to imply some attribute of divinity, but the words directly after this phrase betray such notions. Jesus (pbuh) is clearly speaking of the truth of the message he brings which will lead his followers out of darkness of ignorance, sin and hell and into the light of knowledge, faith and heaven. Therefore the "light of the world" is but a flashlight, a guide to heaven and nothing more.

"I am the Door"

John 10:9 *"I am the door: by me if any man enter in, he shall be saved, and shall go in and out, and find pasture.*
John 10:10 *The thief cometh not, but for to steal, and to kill, and to destroy: I am come that they might have life, and that they might have it more abundantly."*

This passage is another example of Jesus (pbuh) describing himself as the doorway and path to heaven. The words " I am" mystifies his message in some people's mind, but think of it this way, if Jesus (pbuh) is the door to God, it's clear that he is not saying he is God.

"I am the Good Shepherd"

John 10:11 *"I am the good shepherd. The good shepherd lays down his life for the sheep.*
John 10:12 *The hired hand is not the shepherd who owns the sheep. So when he sees the wolf coming, he abandons the sheep and runs away. Then the wolf attacks the flock and scatters it.*
John 10:13 *The man runs away because he is a hired hand and cares nothing for the sheep."*

This is Jesus (pbuh) speaking of his love and devotion to his followers. With these words, Jesus (pbuh) is differentiating himself from someone seeking monetary or worldly gain, but this again has nothing to do with the divinity of Jesus Christ (pbuh). And it is strange that Jesus (pbuh) calls himself "good" when on another occasion he said NONE is "good" except God.

"I am the True Vine"

John 15:1 *"I am the true vine, and my Father is the vine grower.*
John 15:2 *He takes away every branch in me that does not bear fruit, and everyone that does he prunes so that it bears more fruit.*
John 15:3 *You are already pruned because of the word that I spoke to you.*
John 15:4 *Remain in me, as I remain in you. Just as a branch cannot bear fruit on its own unless it remains on the vine, so neither can you unless you remain in me.*
John 15:5 *I am the vine, you are the branches. Whoever remains in me and I in him will bear much fruit, because without me you can do nothing.*
John 15:6 *Anyone who does not remain in me will be thrown out like a branch and wither; people will gather them and throw them into a fire and they will be burned.*

These are beautiful words and they have a beautiful message, but the message does not convey that Jesus (pbuh) is God. On the contrary, it presents the Father as being superior to Jesus (pbuh), as Jesus (pbuh) is the vine and the Father makes him and his followers grow. Over and over again, Jesus (pbuh) stresses that the Father is God and that he is inferior to God.

"I am the Bread of Life"

John 6:35 *Jesus said to them, "I am the bread of life; he who comes to Me will not hunger, and he who believes in Me will never thirst.*
John 6:36 *But I said to you that you have seen Me, and yet do*
not believe.
John 6:37 *All that the Father gives Me will come to Me, and the one who comes to Me I will certainly not cast out.*
John 6:38 *For I have come down from heaven, not to do My own will, but the will of Him who sent Me.*
John 6:39 *This is the will of Him who sent Me, that of all that He has given Me I lose nothing, but raise it up on the last day.*
John 6:40 *For this is the will of My Father, that everyone who beholds the Son and believes in Him will have eternal life, and I Myself will raise him up on the last day."*

When these verses are put into context, it is almost impossible to conclude that Jesus (pbuh) is God. Jesus' (pbuh) constant effort to tell his followers that HE IS NOT GOD seems almost redundant. He speaks of what the Father has "given" him, he says the Father sent him to heaven, and he says that he is NOT doing his will, but the FATHER'S will. Their roles are clearly defined as master and servant. Would any Christian say that Jesus (pbuh) can send the Father somewhere, that Jesus (pbuh) gives anything to the Father, or that Jesus (pbuh) makes the Father follow his will? I doubt that any Christian, be they Trinitarian or not, would say that this is possible. It's obvious that these two beings are not co-equals, when one is ALWAYS subservient to the other.

"I am the Resurrection"

In the story of Jesus (pbuh) raising Lazarus back to life, Martha tells Jesus (pbuh) of her brother's death, because she knows that if Jesus (pbuh) asked God for help, God will give it to him (John 11:22). Jesus (pbuh) tells her that her brother will be raised back to life, but she misunderstood him. She thought that Jesus' (pbuh) was speaking of everyone's resurrection on the Judgment Day.

John 11:25 *Jesus said unto her, I am the resurrection, and the life: he that believeth in me, though he were dead, yet shall he live*
John 11:26 *And whosoever liveth and believeth in me shall never die. Believest thou this?*
John 11:27 *She saith unto him, Yea, Lord: I believe that thou art the Christ, the Son of God, which should come into the world.*

Though some Christians say that Jesus' (pbuh) declaration "I am the resurrection" is a claim towards Jesus (pbuh) being God, it is obvious that Martha did not take his statement in that way. She identifies Jesus (pbuh) as the Christ and the son of God, who asks God for help and receives it. This is her understanding of Jesus (pbuh). If it were that Jesus (pbuh) was God, and she slated Jesus' (pbuh) in his attributes, it is amazing that he is silent on this issue. It is hypocritical to say because Jesus (pbuh) was silent on the issue of people worshipping him (which Martha's sister did in this story) that he is accepting worship as God, but when he is considered to be less than God and he is silent, there is no contradiction there.

His statement that he is the resurrection is to show that he is given power over life and death, just as Elisha, Elijah and

Moses (pbut) were. But by whose authority? It is by God's authority, just as Martha suggested and as Jesus (pbuh) confirms in this very story. Lastly, he explicitly says that he can do NOTHING by HIMSELF (John 5:19) and ALL power is GIVEN TO HIM (Matt. 28:18).

"I am the Way…"

John 14:2 *In my Father's house are many mansions: if [it were] not [so], I would have told you. I go to prepare a place for you. John 14:3 And if I go and prepare a place for you, I will come again, and receive you unto myself; that where I am, [there] ye may be also.*
John 14:4 *And whither I go ye know, and the way ye know.*
John 14:5 *Thomas saith unto him, Lord, we know not whither thou goest; and how can we know the way*
John 14:6 *Jesus saith unto him, I am the way, the truth, and the life: no man cometh unto the Father, but by me.*

It is peculiar to me, why this is considered an example of Jesus' (pbuh) divinity. These verses are self-explanatory in my view. This is reference in to heaven, which is called the Father's house. It is decorated with many mansions and Jesus (pbuh) will go and prepare a place for his disciples. He says to the disciples, you know where I'm going and you know how to get there. Yet Thomas says he doesn't know where Jesus (pbuh) is going and so he doesn't know the way to get there. In response, Jesus (pbuh) says I am the way to heaven. Jesus (pbuh) is the way to the Father. The Father is God. The Father is the goal, not the path to it. Jesus (pbuh) is the path, not the goal according to Jesus' (pbuh) own words.

"I AM"

The reason that so much attention is given to the other seven "I am's" is because of this one. Here is where the Christians might say that Jesus (pbuh) unequivocally declared himself to be God. Or did he?

John 8:56 *Your father Abraham rejoiced to see my day: and he saw it, and was glad.*
John 8:57 *Then said the Jews unto him, Thou art not yet fifty years old, and hast thou seen Abraham?*
John 8:58 *Jesus said unto them, Verily, verily, I say unto you, Before Abraham was, I am.*
John 8:59 *Then took they up stones to cast at him: but Jesus hid himself, and went out of the temple, going through the midst of them, and so passed by.*

To those who are not familiar with the story (Exodus 3:1-16), Moses (pbuh) had stumbled upon a burning bush. From this bush came God's voice giving instructions to Moses (pbuh) to emancipate the children of Israel. God identified himself as "The God of thy father, the God of Abraham, the God of Isaac, and the God of Jacob." After Moses (pbuh) is given instructions, he said the Pharaoh and the Egyptians will ask him, "Who sent him to free the people?" So Moses asks God, Who shall I say has sent me?" In answer to this, God replied "I am that I am," so tell them, "I am" has sent you." The words of Jesus (pbuh) in John are considered by Christians to be a declaration of divinity by Jesus (pbuh) because he repeated the same words, "I am," which God said to Moses (pbuh).

The first point to be made is that immediately following God's answer to what his name is, God answers the question again and again. He answers the question three times. However the last two answers are identical, yet they are different from the first answer. The first answer to what is his name is "I am who I am" (ehyeh asher ehyeh in Hebrew) and "I am" (ehyeh) is the shorten version. This must have been rhetorical, as to say "I am whatever I am," don't worry about my name. The message is the important thing. Because if you ask a man what is your name and he replies "I am who I am," it is apparent that the person doesn't wish to give his name. But God also says his name is "The Lord God of your father, the God of Abraham, the God of Isaac and the God of Jacob" twice, in verse 15 and verse 16. He asserts that this is his name FOREVER. The words "the Lord" are replaced with "Yahweh" or "Jehovah" in some translations.

In Hebrew, it is spelled YHWH. And these letters are in the third person singular form, meaning "He is" whereas ehyeh is first person singular, meaning "I am." It is obvious that "I am" and "He is" are not names. "I am" is used to say, it is not important what my name is and "He is" is the beginning of the phrase "He is God of your father, the God of Abraham..."

So to start with, ehyeh or "I am" is not clearly defined as God's actual name. But for argument sake, let us suppose that this is God's name. A quick glance as Jesus' (pbuh) quote shows that Jesus (pbuh) did not say that "I am" is his name or that he is identical to or identified as "I am." Therefore if you insist that Jesus (pbuh) is declaring divinity by saying these words, you are in fact indicting every person who has ever used these words. If the mere mention of the words "I am" is a claim of divinity, then many have unintentional called themselves God. When someone asks who Ishmael (pbuh) is and I answer that "I am," I am committing blasphemy by these standards. This cannot be the case. Consider

John 9:8 *The neighbours therefore, and they which before had seen him that he was blind, said, Is not this he that sat and begged?*
John 9:9 *Some said, This is he: others [said], He is like him: [but] he said, I am [he].*

If you notice the "he" is in brackets and is not in the original manuscript, but used to help the reader understand the text. Or the brackets are used to help the reader mistakenly believe that only Jesus (pbuh) said "I am." The beggar said the exact same words as Jesus (pbuh) and he said it in the context of his identity, which is more similar to the circumstances surrounding the story in which God said " I am" than Jesus' (pbuh) situation. But no one says he is God or that he is even claiming to be God. And later in this story, the beggar is probed by the Jews about Jesus' (pbuh) identity. He says Jesus (pbuh) is a prophet (John 9:17). Like everyone else who has come into contact or come to know of Jesus (pbuh), the beggar concludes that Jesus (pbuh) is not God, but a man of God.

Another major factor is the actual Greek words used by Jesus (pbuh) are "ego eimi" which is translated as "I am." But the Hebrew Scriptures were translated into Greek long before Jesus (pbuh) was born in the Septuagint and the Greek for "I am" in Exodus 3:14 is "ho on" meaning "the being." Jesus (pbuh) did not equate himself with God because he said "ego eimi" when God said "ho on." In other words, this claim by Christians can work in English, but not in the original language of the gospels, Greek, because the words of Jesus (pbuh) and the words of God are completely different with different meanings. If you ask a Greek speaking person to find in the Bible where Jesus (pbuh) said he was "I am" like God did with Moses (pbuh), he won't be able to find it. He probably does not even know that English speaking Christians are using this to try and prove Jesus' (pbuh) divinity.

Cleverly, Christian apologists have concocted a new explanation for Jesus' use of "ego eimi." They suggest that Jesus was referring to Isaiah 43:10 in which God says "I am" which in the Septuagint is translated "ego eimi." Initially this argument seems plausible. But again, when one fragment of the Trinitarians' claim is explained another emerges in its place.

Isaiah 43:10 *I [am] he (ego eimi): before me there was no God formed, neither shall there be after me.*

The problem is that Jesus (pbuh) and the Holy Spirit formed AFTER the Father. Both Jesus (pbuh) and the Holy Spirit came from the Father. They were either begotten or they proceeded from the Father. Therefore the new approach to the Trinitarian problem is yet another problem.

Nonetheless, in Mark's account of the Jesus' (pbuh) trial, Jesus (pbuh) is asked if he is the son of God. To which he says "I am" (Mark 14:62). Due to the direct questioning of the high priest, one can easily see that in its context, Jesus (pbuh) is not saying that he is God. So what is the context of John 8:56-59? What is Jesus (pbuh) trying to convey to his audience?

Jesus is speaking about Abraham and he said that Abraham REJOICED to see Jesus'(pbut) day and he SAW it and he was glad. This is past tense. What Jesus (pbuh) is saying is that God told Abraham (pbuh) of his coming and God showed him the events that he spoke of, that is how "he saw it" and was rejoiced. The Jews knowing that Jesus (pbuh) couldn't have known Abraham (pbuh) asked him "did he see Abraham?" And Jesus (pbuh) answers, "Before Abraham was, I am." He means before Abraham (pbuh) was on earth, he existed. It is obvious that Jesus (pbuh) is not speaking of his identity, like God did with Moses (pbuh), but he is speaking about time and its correlation to his existence. If Jesus was God, then Abraham saw Jesus (pbut) already and ate with him (Gen. 18:1-8) and Abraham saw Jesus (pbut) at the time of his death. Therefore, the logical explanation is Jesus is saying that he existed before Abraham was on earth and God told Abraham about his mission long before Jesus (pbut) came to this earth. In actual fact, this statement of Jesus (pbuh) should be filed under "Jesus' (pbuh) preexistence."

JESUS' (PBUH) PREEXISTENCE

We can see that with every example used to support the idea of Jesus' (pbuh) divinity, there existed in the Bible examples of others attributed with the same feat or given the same attribute, yet Jesus (pbuh) is the only person considered to be God. Jesus (pbuh) on numerous occasions mentioned his pre-earthly existence. Because he claims to have existed before his time on earth, does that make him God? Is Solomon (pbuh) God? Like Jesus, Solomon (pbut) existed "Ages ago, before the beginning of the heavens and the earth" (Proverbs 8:22-27). The phenomenon Jesus and

Solomon (pbut) speak of is expressed a little more clearly in Jeremiah 1:5.

Jeremiah 1:5 *"Before I formed thee in the belly I knew thee; and before thou camest forth out of the womb I sanctified thee, [and] I ordained thee a prophet unto the nations."*

How did God know Jeremiah before he was in his mother womb and how was Jeremiah a prophet to nations BEFORE he was even born? The answer is simple. Jeremiah, Solomon and Jesus (pbuh) and every human being and animal on earth existed before the universe was here, in the knowledge of God? This is how the Bible could speak of Solomon's (pbuh) existence before the universe was formed, and how Jeremiah was ordained a prophet before birth and how God could show Abraham Jesus' (pbut) days before Jesus (pbuh) came to earth. This would also explain how God knew beforehand and he predestined certain people to be like his son, Jesus (pbuh).

Romans 8:29 *For whom he did foreknow, he also did predestinate to be conformed to the image of his Son, that he might be the firstborn among many brethren.*

One example of Jesus' (pbuh) preexistence, that Trinitarians frequently mentioned is in John 17:5, but since it has been established that Jesus (pbuh) existed along with everyone else in the knowledge of God, let's take a look at the verses preceding John 17:5.

John 17:3 *And this is life eternal, that they might know thee the only true God, and Jesus Christ, whom thou hast sent.*

John 17:4 *I have glorified thee on the earth: I have finished the work which thou gavest me to do.*
John 17:5 *And now, O Father, glorify thou me with thine own self with the glory which I had with thee before the world was.*

We find that Jesus says that eternal life is found in knowing the only true God AND him, the one that GOD SENT. And Jesus continues, "I have FINISHED the work you (God) has given me to do." Then he asks for his reward for his work, which is to glorify him to be in the presence of God, where he had been before the world existed. These verses are in direct contradiction to the divinity of Jesus Christ (pbuh). In Jesus' (pbuh) own words, he places a partition between himself and "the only true God."

ALPHA AND OMEGA

Revelations 1:8 *I am Alpha and Omega, the beginning and the ending, saith the Lord, which is, and which was, and which is to come, the Almighty.*

It is stated that Jesus (pbuh) claimed to be the "alpha and omega" and this is a title of God, thus Jesus is claiming to be God. But is this the title of God? Alpha and omega are the first and last letters of the Greek alphabet. So this is like saying A to Z. And to clarify the meaning, alpha and omega is accompanied by "the beginning and the ending." First of all, Jesus (pbuh) spoke Aramaic and his audience spoke Aramaic, yet he uses Greek letters to convey his message. This is strange, in itself, considering the amount of influence the Greek culture had on shaping the new founded religion of Christianity.

The second problem is that God has no beginning or an ending. He was not created, he always existed and he is eternal. So the claim is flawed and in actual fact contrary to the deification of Jesus (pbuh) because it suggests that he had a beginning and an ending. But of even greater concern should be:

Hebrews 7:3 *Without father, without mother, without descent, having neither beginning of days, nor end of life; but made like unto the Son of God; abideth a priest continually.*

This passage says Melchizedek is MADE like Jesus (pbuh), WITHOUT a beginning or an ending. Let's not forget that the Athanasian Creed says:

22. The Son is of the Father alone; not MADE nor created, but begotten.

This is a clear contradiction in ideas. But the main point is, even if someone interprets "alpha and omega" to mean the beginning and end of life, this title would also applies to Melchizedek. This would give rise to a Quadrinity and there would have to be a new council meeting to include this extraordinary being.

JESUS THE CREATOR

Colossians 1:15 *Who is the image of the invisible God, the firstborn of every creature:*
Colossians 1:16 *For by him were all things created, that are in heaven, and that are in earth, visible and invisible,*

whether they be thrones, or dominions, or principalities, or powers: all things were created by him, and for him:

Jesus (pbuh) is said to be the creator of all things in heaven and on earth, thus giving him the status of God. However the words of John peck at the idea that he is the true creator of everything in heaven and on earth. Jesus (pbuh) is given ALL of his power. Therefore God is the true creator and Jesus (pbuh) is his instrument.

And remember when Jesus (pbuh) was tempted by the devil. It would be rather ridiculous for the devil to offer Jesus (pbuh) the world, when it is already his. The devil TEMPTS Jesus (pbuh) with his own property. This is the property that he created. Jesus (pbuh) being tempted means that he could have succumb to this offer. How could he succumb? If this passage of Colossians is true then Jesus (pbuh) made the devil, who is called the god of this world. So Jesus (pbuh) is the God of the god of this world, yet this lesser god offered Jesus (pbuh) his own possession and Jesus (pbuh) was tempted to accept it.

Let's reflect on the words of God on who is the true creator.

***Isaiah 44:24** Thus saith the LORD, thy redeemer, and he that formed thee from the womb, I [am] the LORD that maketh all [things]; that stretcheth forth the heavens ALONE; that spreadeth abroad the earth BY MYSELF*

THE WORD OF GOD

Jesus (pbuh) is called the word of God. The term "of" signifies possession. The word is God's, not God. When Jesus (pbuh) says that man shall live by every "word of

God" (Luke 4:4), we are not to believe that there is a multitude of gods. We must simply add the apostrophe and declare that everything is God's including his word. Even if one asserts that Jesus (pbuh) was God before he became flesh, when "the word was made flesh" (John 1:14) he became a possession. He was God's word. So if Trinitarians want to insist that he was God as the word of God, then we are back to square one and confronted with multiply gods. Because he is a god possessed by another God.

The funny thing is that if you say Jesus (pbuh) is God and you substitute "word" with "God" in "the word of God," you get that he was "the God of God," which reverses the problem. The answer to one question only causes a new and more damaging problem to arise.

IN THE BEGINNING WAS THE WORD

__John 1:1__ "In beginning was the word..."
(en arche en ho logos)
"and the word was with God..."
(kai ho logos en pros ton theon)
"and the Word was God."
(kai theos en ho logos)

In this passage, "logos" (word) is preceded by the Greek word "ho" meaning "the" and you will notice that there are two different words for God, ton theon and theos.

Trinitarians maintain that Jehovah's Witnesses have changed the Bible and John 1:1 is often quoted as evidence to this claim. This is because in the New World Translation, which is used by Jehovah's Witnesses, the verse reads, "the word was with God and the word was a god." Some Bible translators translate "theos" as "divine" or "a divine being" to give a clearer picture of who "the word" was. The motive for Trinitarians discounting these translations is rather obvious. In order to adhere to the Trinity, they must understand that this verse is speaking of Jesus as "the word" and that he is God Almighty, not simply a divine figure or a lesser god than the Almighty. I have read numerous articles against the New World Translation version but they do not address the difference inferred by the two words "ton theon" and "theos."

It is obvious that these two words have a different meaning. Just as the New World Translation suggests, the "ton theon" is a rendering of the supreme God and "theos" is used as a predicate for someone who is godly in this instance. One does not have to be a Greek scholar to figure this out. The first clue is in the fact that every time the word "logos" is mentioned it has the "ho" with it, to indicate to the reader that this is the same subject in each part of the verse. Yet, the two Greek words for "God" convey to the reader that there are two different subjects.

The word "theos" is used in the New Testament for the supreme God, but this must be understood the same way that "mighty" and "almighty" are both descriptions of God. Because God is almighty, he is also mighty. And because God is the God, he is also godly or a divine being. Yet "mighty" and "theos" can be used for other beings, whereas "ton theon" or "the God" and "almighty" should only be used for the Supreme Being. It must be understood this way because "theos" is also used for the devil (2Cor. 4:4). Is he God Almighty? No. The translators, in this instance, use a lower case "g" for god in describing the devil. In fact

2Corinthians describes the devil as "ho theos" which is a distinction that Jesus is not even afforded in John 1:1. Of course the verse says he is "the god of this age" which, Trinitarians have to acknowledge, indicates that he is "A god." This liberal usage of the word "god" either denotes polytheism or devalues the potency of the word. It allows for people to be called god who do not fit the qualifications, thus its usage must be interpreted by the reader.

When God calls Moses (pbuh) "god" on 2 occasions (Ex. 4:16, 7:1), it is often printed with a lower case "g" because the author makes the distinction between Moses (pbuh) and the supreme God. Though there is no capitalization in the Greek language, in English the translators capitalize "God" when they think a verse is referring to Jesus (pbuh). They are doing more than translating but also interpreting the verse for the reader.

They are making the reader believe that Jesus (pbuh) is synonymous with God Almighty. In Psalms, it says "Ye are gods," with "gods" in lower case, yet there is no lower case in Hebrew or Aramaic. So, how do they determine what is capitalized and what is not? The translators decide for you, when this is not his job.

Now equipped with the knowledge that "god" in the Bible is not always referring to the God Almighty, let's look again at John 1:1. The second part of the verse has the words "ton theon" meaning "The God," but none of the translators add the word "the." Aside from the fact that the word for "the," "ho," is used repeatedly to identify that the same person is being spoken of, the word "ton," also meaning "the," is omitted in this instance to avoid the reader questioning whether or not "The Word" and "the God" are identical. But the phrase, "the word was with God" betrays the translator's intent. If there is any indication that there is more than one being mentioned in this text, it is this phrase. This is the cement to the argument. How can Jesus (pbuh) be WITH himself? Ton theon is the totality of God and Jesus (pbuh) is described in the verse to be with him and he was godly or divine.

I am puzzled that the contradiction that "the words was with God" and "the word was God" is so well known and so apparent, and both phrases are accepted as being true. If words have any meaning, then this is one of the most obvious contradictions in the Bible. The word "with" means that there is someone and there is someone else accompanying them. One cannot be "with" himself. But Trinitarians have to believe that one person can be "with himself," in order to remain monotheists and accept this verse as being true.

I heard a lecture from Christian apologist William Lane Craig in which he said that all three parts of the Trinity of God love each other and this love is different from the God of Islam, because the God of Islam could, in the beginning, only loved himself. But this argument again ignores the meaning of words, like the words "love" and "each other." If the Trinitarians believe in one God and the parts of the Trinity are collectively AND separately God and they loved each other, then they are, like the God of Islam, loving themselves. If the Trinitarian insists that loving each other is different from loving themselves, like Mr. Craig did, then he is speaking of polytheism. The belief in three separate divine beings that love each other is belief in three gods.

Does this sentence make sense: The one God loved each other? Not at all. But this sentence does: The three gods loved each other. So, the Trinitarians can say that God is one, but they cannot say that he loved each other. Or the Trinitarian can say that they loved each other, but he cannot say that they are one being. He can have it one way or the other, but he cannot have it both. In like manner, they cannot say that Jesus (pbuh) is with God and Jesus (pbuh) is God, because those words do not make sense.

If we read the verse again, it starts off as rather vague and abstract. "In the beginning..." Someone may ask, "in the beginning of what?" It is in Genesis 1:1, where we find that this is speaking of the beginning of creation. So, before creation, there was the word? He was probably with the "wisdom."

Proverbs 8:22-30 says God possessed her (speaking of wisdom as a woman) before his creating of anything in heaven or on earth. "Ton Theon" possessed him and her before creation and he used his wisdom and his word to make the universe.

I submit that in the beginning of creation, God created everything by his wisdom and his word. Genesis says over and over again, that "God said..." and the thing came into being. It is clear that Jesus (pbuh) is not in this story, but it is actually God using his WORDS and they manifest. Everything and everyone on earth is God's word. Jesus (pbuh) is called God's word, to illuminate his miraculous birth, even though Jesus (pbuh) is the word of God just as everyone else is. The only difference is that God spoke him into being without the process by which other people are born. And due to this, Paul erroneously concluded that if Jesus (pbuh) was the word of God and God created everything by his word, then Jesus (pbuh) created everything. And later John perpetuated this misunderstanding.

They did not take into account that God has more than one word. So it is just as plausible (or implausible) to suggest that Adam (pbuh) or Eve created everything, because undoubtedly they are also the words of God. So too was the moon and the sun and the night and the day and so on.

What is strange is that the Holy Spirit is nowhere to be found in John 1:1. I would contend that this is because he is not God, thus easily absent from this picture. Or his absence may be due to the fact that John is not truly the author of this text. It has long been debated that this verse possesses a poetic language that is not present in any of the remaining verses of this gospel or the other books of John. The reliability of crucial Bible verses is in question constantly by Bible scholars. And what is found should not be surprising at this point.

St Augustine, an early author and authority for Christianity, admitted that he had found great similitude to John 1:1 written long before Jesus (pbuh) or John walked this earth.

"Thou procuredst for me, by means of one puffed up with most unnatural pride, certain books of the Platonists, translated from Greek into Latin. And therein I read, not indeed in the very words, but to the very same purpose, enforced by many and divers reasons, that In the beginning was the Word, and the Word was with God, and the Word was God: the Same was in the beginning with God" (Augustine, Confessions, book VII)

We must revisit the notion that the Greeks and their views of God had a profound impact on the most important tenets of the Christian faith.

THE FATHER AND I ARE ONE

When asked, when Jesus (pbuh) expressed equality with God, the Christian might say when Jesus says "the Father and I are one." One might ask "one what?" Does Jesus (pbuh) say that he is one in nature with God? Most Christians believe that this is what Jesus (pbuh) meant in this instance. But they are mistaken.

The primary problem with the claim that this phrase is indicative of Jesus' (pbuh) divinity is due to the fact that it is never quoted in its context. If this story is given in its entirety, it is clear that Jesus (pbuh) did not say he was God and it can, in no way, be taken as such. The story reads as follows.

John 10:24 *So the Jews gathered around him and said to him, "How long are you going to keep us in suspense? 11 If you are the Messiah, tell us plainly."*
John 10:25 *Jesus answered them, "I told you and you do not believe. The works I do in my Father's name testify to me.*
John 10:26 *But you do not believe, because you are not among my sheep.*
John 10:27 *My sheep hear my voice; I know them, and they follow me.*

John 10:28 *I give them eternal life, and they shall never perish. No one can take them out of my hand.*
John 10:29 *My Father, who has given them to me, is greater than all, and no one can take them out of the Father's hand.*
John 10:30 *The Father and I are one.*
John 10:31 *The Jews again picked up rocks to stone him.*
John 10:32 *Jesus answered them, "I have shown you many good works from my Father. For which of these are you trying to stone me?"*
John 10:33 *The Jews answered him, "We are not stoning you for a good work but for blasphemy. You, a man, are making yourself God."*
John 10:34 *Jesus answered them, "Is it not written in your law, 'I said, "You are gods"'?*
John 10:35 *If it calls them gods to whom the word of God came, and scripture cannot be set aside,*
John 10:36 *can you say that the one whom the Father has consecrated and sent into the world blasphemes because I said, 'I am the Son of God'?*
John 10:37 *If I do not perform my Father's works, do not believe me;*
John 10:38 *but if I perform them, even if you do not believe me, believe the works, so that you may realize (and understand) that the Father is in me and I am in the Father."*
John 10:39 *(Then) they tried again to arrest him; but he escaped from their hands*

The Jews came around Jesus (pbuh) accusing him of speaking ambiguously. They contended that Jesus (pbuh) hadn't clearly stated whether he is the Christ or not. Jesus (pbuh) denies this claim. He said I told you already but you won't believe me because you are not my sheep. My sheep hear and believe me. Then he says he has given his sheep eternal life because they following him. And Jesus (pbuh) says he will see to it that no one takes them off track. He says that the Father has given them to him and the Father is "GREATER THAN ALL" and the Father will also see to it that they stay on the right path. In this, in keeping the believers on the right path, he and the Father are one. He is not saying he is one in nature with the Father, but in PURPOSE.

It is as if two men from separate sides of the earth are propagating their faith. They are one in their purpose to spread the message of truth, but they are two different people.

So the Jews go to stone him for blasphemy. They charge that Jesus (pbuh) is saying he is God, by saying "The Father and I are one." Notice that they understand that the Father is God. What does Jesus (pbuh) say? They have already accused him of being ambiguous. If he is God, what can he say but, "I must tell the truth, I am God?" Was he too scared to tell the truth? At the end of this incident, he ran and escaped from them anyway. If he was scared he might as well tell the truth and then ran away.

Jesus (pbuh), instead of affirming that he is God, denies the charge. He says the scripture calls other people gods, but he only said that he is the son of God. Notice that Jesus (pbuh) is implying that the son of God is something less than God, not equal to God. In essence he is saying, how can you find fault in what I say, when the scriptures you believe in say something much more on the level of blasphemy? Then he affirms again his oneness with God in purpose and they attack him and Jesus (pbuh) escaped.

Someone my say, "Jesus said he is in the Father and the Father in him," so this is something to declare Jesus' (pbuh) divinity. Or they say that the Greek word for "one" used in John 10:30 is "hen" and it is a word personifying the meaning of one in nature, not purpose. However Jesus (pbuh) says of the disciples

John 17:21 *That they all may be one; as thou, Father, [art] in me, and I in thee, that they also may be one in us: that the world may believe that thou hast sent me.*
John 17:22 *And the glory which thou gavest me I have given them; that they may be one, even as we are one:*
John 17:23 *I in them, and thou in me, that they may be made perfect in one; and that the world may know that thou hast sent me, and hast loved them, as thou hast loved me.*

These verses use the same Greek word "hen." So if you declare that being one with the Father or being in the Father and the Father being in you means you are God, then the disciple must be placed in the godhead, also. In Matthew 10:40, Jesus (pbuh) says if you receive the disciples you receive Jesus (pbuh) and you receive God. Does this mean that they all are one? Jesus (pbuh) clarifies this point in Mark 9:37, where he says that if you receive him, you are not actually receiving him, but the one that sent him, God. The disciples and Jesus (pbuh) are only tools of God used to bring people to him. They are all one in purpose, but in nature. Luke 4:32 says that all that believed were one in heart and soul. This is in the same vein as the words of Jesus (pbuh). Jesus (pbuh) is in no way including himself in the oneness of God. His every word is in opposition to this premise.

The gospel of John, which contains the famous, "the Father and I are one" verse, often draws the distinction between these two beings. For example, we find in this gospel that the Father is greater than Jesus (pbuh) (John 14:28) and that the Father and Jesus (pbuh) are described as two witnesses to the same event (John 8:18).

Also wrapped your mind around the idea that Jesus (pbuh) is God, but when the Jews picked up stones to cast at him for blasphemy, "God" escaped and hid.

JEWS WANTED TO STONE HIM

The fact that the Jews wanted to stone Jesus (pbuh) on several occasions is given as proof that Jesus (pbuh) was claiming to be God. Some Christians say that the Jews were right to believe he was equating himself with God, but this was not blasphemy because he actually was God. The problem with this is they are assuming that the Jews understood Jesus (pbuh). It has to be that the Jews did not understand what Jesus (pbuh) said because if they did understand him it would make no sense then to have him killed. In the instances in which the Jews accused him of equating himself with God, Jesus (pbuh) refuted their accusations. He, in essence is saying, no you are misunderstanding me. Jesus (pbuh) says he came for the lost sheep of the house of Israel (Matt. 15:24). When Jesus (pbuh) says my sheep hear my voice and follow me, he is speaking of those who understand him. But to those Jews attacking him, he says they are not his sheep and they don't hear his voice.

Obviously they can literally hear him speaking, he means "seeing they see not, hearing they hear not, neither do they understand" (Matt13:13). Therefore the Jews that rejected him did not understand him. Mark Chapter four is almost entirely dedicated to the premise that his message is for those with understanding. Jesus (pbuh) said if you don't accept the message, then you do not understand the message. Another sign of their misunderstanding is the fact that Jesus (pbuh) says he came to fulfill the laws and commandments (Matt. 5:17), yet he is captured and imprisoned for breaking the commandments.

Obviously they misunderstood him. Many times they misunderstood him purposely, probably because of the manner in which he admonished the behavior of people or the harsh name calling of Jesus (pbuh) to the Jews in the Bible, i.e. fools, wicked and adulterous generation, generation of vipers.

What is strange is that the people who brought up lie after lie to have Jesus (pbuh) executed, are only given credibility when it is in support of Jesus' (pbuh) divinity. This is no coincidence. Are not these the same people who captured Jesus (pbuh), who gave false witness against Jesus (pbuh), who accused him of blasphemy before the high priest (Matt. 26:65), later changing the charge before Pontius Pilate to accuse Jesus (pbuh) of claiming to be "King of the Jews" (Luke 23:2)? Are not these the people who chose to free a murderer in order to have Jesus (pbuh) slain (Luke 23:16-19)? Are they not the people who orchestrated a trial in the middle of the night and the early morning to silence

Jesus' (pbuh) message, because they felt it expedient that Jesus (pbuh) die in order to save their nation from being further trampled by the Romans (John 11:46-53, 18:14)?

Are they not the people who swore by themselves and their children that Jesus (pbuh) deserved death for all these trumped up charges (Matt 27:25)? In other words, they were desperate. They are looking for any excuse to shut Jesus (pbuh) up. When the Jews brought these false witnesses to corroborate the claim of blasphemy, Jesus (pbuh) said he spoke openly to the world.

He taught in the temple and the synagogues (John 18:20). So he wants to know why can't they bring some actually witnesses to this crime. It's because the charge of blasphemy against him was a lie. He never claimed to be God, to be equal to God, or to be God's actual son.

Jesus (pbuh) says that the Jews had stoned and killed other prophets before him (Matt. 23:37). Obviously these prophets were true, yet the Jews had them killed because they misunderstood them. So they also misunderstood Jesus (pbuh). The understanding of those who opposed his every word and action can be of little value assuming that their opposition was incorrect and Jesus (pbuh) was true.

My Lord and My God

John 20:28 *And Thomas answered and said unto him, My Lord and my God.*
John 20:29 *Jesus saith unto him, Thomas, because thou hast seen me, thou hast believed: blessed [are] they that have not seen, and [yet] have believed.*

Upon initial review, one may possibly surmise that Thomas is calling Jesus (pbuh) God and Jesus (pbuh) is acknowledging this fact. It seems cut and dry. Had it been so cut and dry, this verse would have been mentioned earlier and used as clear proof that Jesus (pbuh) was called God in his lifetime and he accepted this title. But it should be obvious by now, that every verse given is not always what it seems. We must remember to quote in context. What was the context of these words by Thomas and Jesus (pbuh)?

First we must remember that Thomas is famously called "Doubting Thomas." Why is he given this nickname? Did he doubt the divinity of Jesus Christ (pbuh)? For the answer, we must summons John to testify. We need not look any further than four verses ahead

John 20:24 *But Thomas, one of the twelve, called Didymus, was not with them when Jesus came.*
John 20:25 *The other disciples therefore said unto him, We have seen the Lord. But he said unto them, Except I shall see in his hands the print of the nails, and put my finger into the print of the nails, and thrust my hand into his side, I will not believe.*
John 20:26 *And after eight days again his disciples were within, and Thomas with them: [then] came Jesus, the doors being shut, and stood in the midst, and said, Peace [be] unto you.*
John 20:27 *Then saith he to Thomas, Reach hither thy finger, and behold my hands; and reach hither thy hand, and thrust [it] into my side: and be not faithless, but believing.*

The gospel of John testifies that Thomas is called Doubting Thomas because the other disciples saw and spoke with Jesus (pbuh) after his alleged crucifixion and they told Thomas about this encounter, but Thomas said he would not believe them until he saw and touch Jesus (pbuh) himself. Thomas doubts that the other disciples saw a physical Jesus (pbuh). He or they make no mention of the divinity of Jesus (pbuh). So when he saw Jesus (pbuh), he touched Jesus (pbuh) and Jesus (pbuh) said don't doubt but believe. Don't doubt what? Believe what? He is telling Thomas not to doubt, but believe the accounts of the other disciples, that he is a physical being, still possessing his wounds. Thomas responded "my lord and my god."

It is clear that this is not even a good example to be used by Trinitarians. This is a response of exclamation by Thomas. He is overjoyed or in disbelief. People every day and all day make similar cries, like "Oh God!" Is anyone declared God from such a statement? Not ever. So when Jesus (pbuh) says now Thomas is a believer it is not because Thomas called him God, but because now he is no longer a doubter but a believer as to what the other disciples told him. And Jesus (pbuh) could tell this perhaps by the look on his face and for certain by his words of astonishment, "my lord and my god"

We are told by Paul in 1Corinthians 8:6 that "there is one God, the Father…and one Lord, Jesus Christ." So we realize that the Father is God and Jesus is the lord. Unless Jesus (pbuh) is also the Father, we must conclude that even if Thomas was calling for God, that he was speaking of the Father and not Jesus (pbuh). The title of lord has been defined as someone's leader or master and it is used for those not considered to a deity by anyone. In 1Thessalonians

1:2, we find the phrase "God our Father and the Lord Jesus." Even in the famous verse of Romans, we see the differentiation of the Lord and God.

Romans 14:11 *For it is written, '"As I live,' says the Lord, 'to me every knee will bow. Every tongue will confess to God.'"*

The words of Thomas separate the two persons mention with the word "and." This is apparently in tune with the other writers of the New Testament as documented above. With this in mind, it is again obvious that he is not addressing Jesus (pbuh), but speaking out of excitement. Lastly, the author of John ends this story by solidifying the fact that Thomas is not regarding Jesus (pbuh) as God, that Jesus' (pbuh) questioning is not to convince Thomas of his divinity and that Jesus' (pbuh) silence about Thomas' response were not approval of Thomas' supposed testimony that Jesus (pbuh) is God, in John 20:30-31.

John 20:30 *And many other signs truly did Jesus in the presence of his disciples, which are not written in this book:*
John 20:31 *But these are written, that ye might believe that Jesus is the Christ, the Son of God; and that believing ye might have life through his name.*

The author says that THIS and many other signs were used to convince people that Jesus (pbuh) is the Christ, not the Jesus (pbuh) is God Almighty. Throughout the gospels it is apparent that Jesus (pbuh) is the Christ and the son of God. What is not apparent, and what the Trinitarians wish John said was that these signs were written that ye might believe Jesus (pbuh) is God. But it is nowhere to be found. So this story cannot be used to claim the divinity of Jesus (pbuh).

PROPHECIES OF JESUS (PBUH)

There have been claims of hundreds of prophecies of Jesus (pbuh) present in the Old Testament. Of course, the original followers of the Old Testament, the Jews would disagree and refute every claim. Several of these prophecies have unraveling in this book, but if the Old Testament does foretell the coming of Jesus (pbuh), this is not an evidence for Jesus' (pbuh) divinity.

Muslims have produced evidence that Muhammad (pbuh) is prophesied of in the Bible. This is not suggested without debate. But no learned Christian will debate that Elijah (pbuh) was prophesied to come back (Mal. 4:5) and he did return as John the Baptist (pbuh) (Matt. 11:12-13, 17:10-13, Luke 1:17), which nullifies the argument that prophecies and their fulfillment, means someone is God.

JESUS (PBUH) TAKEN TO HEAVEN

Some Christians hold that because Jesus (pbuh) ascended into heaven that he is God. Whatever the reasoning behind this may be, if this phenomenon can be showed to have happened before or after Jesus (pbuh), it would disqualify this claim as proof of Jesus' (pbuh) divinity. The main difficulty in showing that others have ascended to heaven in the Bible to a Christian is that in order to prove this I must contradict one of Jesus' (pbuh) declarations. He said that no one has entered heaven (John 3:13).

Yet Enoch was taken into heaven according to the Bible.

Genesis 5:23 *And all the days of Enoch were three hundred sixty and five years:*
Genesis 5:24 *And Enoch walked with God: and he was not; for God took him.*

Because of the words of Jesus (pbuh), which boldly state that no one has entered heaven, Christians are forced to understand this story of Enoch to simply mean that he died. However if one observes the entire chapter of Genesis carefully, they find that this chapter is a documentation of important people of the Bible and their age at the time of their demise. It speaks of Adam (pbuh) and says he was "nine hundred and thirty years: and he died." Seth was "nine hundred and twelve years: and he died."

…and he died.
…and he died.
…and he died.
…and he died.
…and he died.

Interestingly enough when we arrive at Enoch's end, he "walked with God: and he was not; for God took him." Where did God take him? Where did he walk with God? Does this verse say he died? No, he was taken by God. This obviously has a meaning other than death. By simple deduction, we know that God is in heaven, Enoch didn't die, but "he was not," and God took him. Enoch must have been taken to heaven. To further illustrate this point, the author of Genesis continues his list with two more people and it says "and he died" for both of them. It is a deliberate distinction. And we may get a clear picture of just how Enoch "was not, for God took Him" from the story of Elijah's (pbuh) rapture into heaven.

2Kings 2:11 *And it came to pass, as they still went on, and talked, that, behold, there appeared a chariot of fire, and horses of fire, and parted them both asunder; and Elijah went up by a whirlwind into heaven.*
2Kings 2:12 *And Elisha saw it, and he cried, My father, my father, the chariot of Israel, and the horsemen thereof. And he saw him no more: and he took hold of his own clothes, and rent them in two pieces.*

We see here that Elisha and Elijah (pbut) were walking along and a chariot of fire split them apart and Elijah (pbuh) is whisked into heaven. Perhaps this is how Enoch was taken by God and was no more. But the more important point is that this is a clear story of a person being taken into heaven. Unlike the ending of life for Enoch, Elijah (pbuh) is clearly stated to have been taken to heaven and Elisha (pbuh) is a witness to this happening. And there are other instances of people taken to heaven.

We have just established that Elijah (pbuh) is taken to heaven. Now in Matt 17:2-3 there is the story of Jesus speaking with Elijah, who is also called Elias, and Moses (pbut), both of whom had long since left this earth. Moses' (pbuh) death is documented in the Bible (Deut.34:7), and it is clear that after his death he is with Elijah (pbuh), which is in heaven. And there is also, the story of the rich man, who is simmering in hell and Lazarus, the beggar, who can see and converse with the rich man from Heaven (Luke 16:19-31). From the story, we find that this is not after the Last Day because the rich man mentions his brothers who are still on earth and in need of guidance. Some may conclude that this is a parable and not a literal story, but this does not negate the implications made by Jesus (pbuh) that some people will be in heaven and others in hell after their death and before the Last day. To clarify this we have Paul in 2Corinthians 12:2 speaking of a man who went to heaven

2Corinthians 12:2 *I knew a man in Christ above fourteen years ago, (whether in the body, I cannot tell; or whether out of the body, I cannot tell: God knoweth;) such an one caught up to the third heaven.*

With this we can conclude that being taken to and living in heaven is not exclusively for the divine and that Jesus (pbuh) must have been mistaken when he said that no one has been to Heaven. But God does not make mistakes.

WHEN YOU SEE ME, YOU SEE THE FATHER

John 14:9 *"he that hath seen me hath seen the Father"*

John 5:37 *And the Father himself, which hath sent me, hath borne witness of me. Ye have neither heard his voice at any time, nor seen his shape.*

How can someone possibly reconcile these two verses? At face value, it may appear that Jesus (pbuh) is claiming to be the Father in the first quote, but in the second verse, Jesus (pbuh) speaks of two distinct persons. Not to mention that all the disciples and people around Jesus (pbuh) heard his voice and saw him with their bodily eyes, thus disqualifying him from being the Father. It is impossible to believe both these verses, literally. Jesus (pbuh) had to be speaking metaphorical in one of these verses. John 5:37 is clear and is echoed throughout the Bible including John 1:18 which says:

John 1:18 *No man hath seen God at any time, the only begotten Son, which is in the bosom of the Father, he hath declared him.*

From this simple verse, we find that the "son" and "God" are not one, but distinct from one another. And that Jesus (pbuh) was not God, before, during or after his time on earth. But we must still explore the meaning of John 14:9 in its context. In Chapter 14, Jesus (pbuh) is discussing the place he will set aside in heaven for his follower. But these words are too much for his disciple, Philip, to understand. Philip cuts to the chase. He says "just show us the Father" and then he will believe.

John 14:9 *Jesus saith unto him, Have I been so long time with you, and yet hast thou not known me, Philip? he that hath seen me hath seen the Father; and how sayest thou [then], Shew us the Father?*
John 14:10 *Believest thou not that I am in the Father, and the Father in me? the words that I speak unto you I speak not of myself: but the Father that dwelleth in me, he doeth the works.*

Now in context, we see once again that Jesus (pbuh) is not saying that he is God or the Father, but that he only says and does what the Father commands him to do. Because he is the Father's representative to humanity, he personifies righteousness and good, which will lead people to the Father. This is also how he is the "way" to the Father. Those who are righteous or those who are of God have seen God, in the Biblical sense, because "he that doeth evil hath not seen God" (3 John 1:11). Obviously, this and Jesus' (pbuh) words are not literal but metaphorical for those on the wrong path and those on the right path.

This leads us to the image of God.

JESUS (PBUH) IS GOD'S IMAGE

Colossians 1:15 *Who is the image of the invisible God, the firstborn of every creature:*

Hebrews 1:3 *Who being the brightness of [his] glory, and the express image of his person, and upholding all things by the word of his power, when he had by himself purged our sins, sat down on the right hand of the Majesty on high*

I would like to ponder the words "image of the invisible." Could this possibly be taken literally? Can something invisible have an image? We are given a hint to the Biblical understanding of God's image in Genesis.

Genesis 1:26 *"And God said, Let us make man in our image, after our likeness."*

"Image" in this verse is not literal, but metaphorical. Obviously, we don't all look alike and we definitely don't all look like God. The words "after our likeness" helps establish that God's image is that of righteousness and piety which God bestows upon man. Therefore if Jesus (pbuh) is God's image, he is the living example which we must follow. It must also be cemented in our minds that an apostrophe "s" and "of" means ownership. So if Jesus (pbuh) is God's image or the image of God, he can't be God, for he is God's possession. And Christians are warned in the Bible about understanding God's image literally.

Romans 1:23 *And changed the glory of the uncorruptible God into an image made like to corruptible man.*

Jesus (pbuh) is also differentiated from God in the verses of Colossians and Hebrews. In the first passage, he is called the "firstborn" of creation, yet God has no beginning. And in the second passage, the author has Jesus (pbuh) on the right side of God's throne of "the Majesty on high."

JESUS (PBUH) THE MANIFESTATION OF GOD?

1 Timothy 3:16 *And without controversy great is the mystery of godliness: God was manifest in the flesh, justified in the Spirit, seen of angels, preached unto the Gentiles, believed on in the world, received up into glory.*

The King James Version of the Bible lives by the motto, "the customer is always right." I say this because in just about every instance in which Jesus' (pbuh) divinity is alluded to, Biblical scholars find and correct some discrepancies in almost all versions of the Bible, except the King James Version. His version blatantly compromises the truth to sell the goods to the customer. The earliest and most reliable manuscripts of the Bible do not have the word "God" in this verse at all, but the word "he." This slight change is stupendous when put in perspective. When we add the "he," we find that this is in no way referring to God becoming a human being, but this is solely speaking about Jesus (pbuh). It is merely describing the beginning of Jesus' (pbuh) earthly existence. It would be of some benefit to Trinitarians if the apparent interpolation was in the original manuscripts, but honest Bible scholars and translators have admitted that "God" was placed in this verse incorrectly. This is another discovery documented in Sir Isaac Newton's textual criticism of the Bible from 1754, yet this verse is, to this day, translated incorrectly. Some Bibles make the corrections but only in the footnotes. Is this sufficient when we are confronted with the task of examining the nature of God Almighty and the faith of billions of people? How often do people read footnotes and commentaries? How often do people read, period? To hide such important information or to place it in the fine print is unacceptable.

Part V

MORE PROOF THAT JESUS (PBUH) IS NOT GOD

JESUS (PBUH) HAS A GOD

<u>Matthew 27:46</u> *And about the ninth hour Jesus cried with a loud voice, saying, Eli, Eli, lama sabbachthani? that is to say, My God, my God, why hast thou forsaken me?*

This passage is from Jesus (pbuh) on the cross. When I encountered this verse in my reading and research, I was taken aback. When I let these words spin around in my head, I could not grasp anybody on earth reading this and not simultaneously questioning the premise that Jesus Christ (pbuh) is God. As I read through the gospels, I recognized evidence that Jesus (pbuh) was not God and to me this verse was the icing on the cake. I have in numerous debates mention Matthew 27:46 but at varying times during the debate. I often use this at the end of the debate as a selling point. I have used it in the midst of a debate to help me redirect my focus or my opponent's focus. And it can be used in the beginning of the debate to gauge a person's sincerity or their knowledge of their faith. Many times Christians have never heard this verse before, if they are not avid readers. Silence on this verse might be construed as a deliberate omission on the part of a minister.

The Christians I have debated about this verse always seem to fall in two categories. They are in denial as to its meaning and shrug its meaning off and the entire line of questioning off or they concoct a fantastic explanation as to why Jesus (pbuh) said this. This explanation is usually not to answer my inquiry, but to satisfy those listeners who are believers already. And this response is normally from some publication and not their understanding. This is because its explanation is not understandable. I declare that in order for this verse to be believed in congruency with Jesus (pbuh) being God is impossible and even a fantastic explanation will not make it work. This is because the words attributed to Jesus (pbuh) in this verse contradict ever possible explanation of his divinity.

The first of the damaging evidence is the fact that Jesus (pbuh) has a God. He says "My God, My God." If you still believe Jesus (pbuh) is God after reading this, then you must concede that he is not the supreme God. There is no way around this problem. But of course, many have come up with an explanation. They say, "this is Jesus the man talking, not Jesus the God." Jesus (pbuh) the man can have a God and pray to him and so on.

This is rather deceitful. They go through great pains to say that Jesus (pbuh) was sinless, Jesus (pbuh) was a ransom for sin, Jesus (pbuh) was born without the Original Sin, Jesus (pbuh) could have saved himself from death, and he was begotten of God. All of this is in an effort to show that Jesus (pbuh) is God.

But when they are confronted with Jesus' (pbuh) humanity, the story changes. They say he has two natures that he switches on and off, without rhyme or reason. The only alternative for Trinitarians is to conclude that Jesus (pbuh) is God up above and he is controlling the man on earth. But how would this explanation satisfy the Trinitarian. These explanations were devised in an effort to explain why Jesus (pbuh) said that he had a God, but when they solve one problem they create a new one. Their proposed solution contradicts the second damaging factor of this verse, "Why have you forsaken me?"

This totally negates the position that Jesus (pbuh) is God and he is manipulating the man below and that he has a dual nature which switches on and off on a whim, because he says that God forsook him. Was Jesus' (pbuh) lying or gesturing? Jesus (pbuh) never sinned, so he couldn't be lying. Did Jesus (pbuh) make a mistake from his own human weakness and assert that God deserted him? How could a man so in tune with God make such an error? Was it not him who said, God hears him ALWAYS? But this is not the first time Jesus (pbuh) has supposedly made a mistake. In Mark, Jesus (pbuh) is hungry and seeing a fig tree from afar and he goes to the tree for figs for food. But when he gets to the tree, he finds that the tree has no fruit because it is not the season for the fruit. In response to the sight of the fruitless tree, Jesus (pbuh) cursed the tree (Mark 11:12-22).

In this story, we must understand Jesus' (pbuh) hunger to be a human weakness. Jesus (pbuh) contempt for this tree is also human weakness. Consider that according to God's law, the tree was not supposed to bear fruit at that time, so out of anger and hunger, Jesus (pbuh) invoked his power of divinity. It is evident from this verse that the human Jesus (pbuh) is in control of his divine powers, which would contradict that idea that Jesus (pbuh) from above was controlling the man Jesus (pbuh). Even if this were the case, can it be possible to believe that God's power is subordinate to the weakness of hunger, anger and lack of understanding of a man? In the case of the dual nature of Jesus, can we surmise that Jesus' (pbuh) divinity was guided by a human's weakness? This would be a discredit and a disservice to God. In fact, it is blasphemous. This kind of thinking is given to use in the Old Testament. A drunken Noah (pbuh) curses his innocent grandchild for the iniquity of his son and God upholds this curse (Gen. 9:21-27). Jacob (pbuh) bribes his brother, lies and deceives his blind father to steal his brother's birthright. And God upholds the stolen firstborn right of Jacob (pbuh). God is just and true. He does not act on the behests of those who, through mistake or mischievous behavior due to human weakness, ask for his assistance. With this in mind and the fact that the Father is actually the puppeteer moving Jesus (pbuh) we must conclude that at the moment on the cross when Jesus (pbuh) cried out, Jesus (pbuh) felt destitute and deserted by God. Therefore, he was not God and according to Jesus (pbuh), God was not even with him.

It is rather strange that Jesus (pbuh) says that his God was not with him, but maybe he meant the Father. So where was the Holy Spirit? Well if the Holy Spirit is the Comforter, then he was not with Jesus (pbuh) either, because Jesus (pbuh) said that the Comforter WILL NOT come, until Jesus (pbuh) leaves. When Jesus (pbuh) leaves he will SEND the Comforter (John 16:7). It seems the godheads of the Trinity were far removed from each other for a time.

On another occasion, Jesus (pbuh) is speaking with Mary Magdalene and:

John 20:17 *Jesus saith unto her, Touch me not; for I am not yet ascended to my Father: but go to my brethren, and say unto them, I ascend unto my Father, and your Father; and [to] my God, and your God.*

This passage speaks volumes about Jesus (pbuh) being the son of God and about his supposed divinity. We must first understand that the four titles mentioned by Jesus (pbuh) are all for the same person. That is to say, his Father and her Father are the same being, his God and her God are the same being, and their God and their father are the same being. This means that his relationship with his Father and his God can be equated to that of an ordinary person. Thus he is not a unique son of God, as mentioned earlier and most assuredly he has a God, which he worships and fears just as any righteous servant of God does. To pronounce divinity upon such a person would only imply the belief in more than one God. And there is further evidence to prove that Jesus (pbuh) has a God.

Romans 15:6 *so that with one heart and mouth you may glorify the God and Father of our Lord Jesus Christ.*

2Corinthians 1:3 *Praise be to the God and Father of our Lord Jesus Christ, the Father of compassion and the God of all comfort,*

2Corinthians 11:31 *The God and Father of the Lord Jesus, who is to be praised forever, knows that I am not lying.*

Ephesians 1:3 *Praise be to the God and Father of our Lord Jesus Christ, who has blessed us in the heavenly realms with every spiritual blessing in Christ.*

Colossians 1:3 *We always thank God, the Father of our Lord Jesus Christ, when we pray for you,*

1Peter 1:3 *Praise be to the God and Father of our Lord Jesus Christ! In his great mercy he has given us new birth into a living hope through the resurrection of Jesus Christ from the dead*

Yet in Hebrews, we have Jesus (pbuh) being called god by God.

Hebrews 1:8 *But unto the Son [he saith], Thy throne, O God, [is] for ever and ever: a sceptre of righteousness [is] the sceptre of thy kingdom.*

I would hope readers of this will keep in mind the explanation given earlier about human beings being called god in the Bible, because if this is taken literal, it can only hurt the Trinitarians' case. Because the very next verse nullifies the doctrine of the Trinity and renders those with the belief that Jesus (pbuh) is God to be polytheists. God says this god that he is speaking of has a god.

Hebrews 1:9 *Thou hast loved righteousness, and hated iniquity; therefore God, [even] thy God, hath anointed thee with the oil of gladness above thy fellows.*

To say at this point that it is obvious that Jesus (pbuh) has a God is an understatement. It is a fact that the Bible records, on numerous occasions, the disciples saying Jesus has a God, Jesus (pbuh) saying he has a God and God Almighty saying Jesus (pbuh) has a God. This should give Trinitarians pause as to the validity of their claims. But they are not easily dissuaded from their beliefs.

JESUS (PBUH) IN HIS GLORY AND ESSENCE

Some Trinitarians maintain that Jesus (pbuh) had a God, in whom he served and worshipped, only as a human being on earth. In his heavenly glory and essence, Jesus (pbuh) takes his true position alongside the Father. But we must first understand that even in his glory, Jesus (pbuh) is only sitting at the right hand of the Father (Matt. 26:64, Col. 3:1). He doesn't occupy the king's throne, but the throne of the prince (of peace). He is like the right hand man of God, not actually God. Nonetheless, we find in John's vision or DREAM of Jesus (pbuh) in his glory and essence, Jesus (pbuh) continues to insist that he has a God, again rendering the puppeteer theory false. It also gives rise to the implication of two separate deities of varying power and strength.

Revelations 1:1 *The revelation of Jesus Christ, which God gave him to show his servants what must soon take place. He made it known by sending his angel to his servant John,*

Revelations 1:6 *and has made us to be a kingdom and priests to serve his God and Father to him be glory and power for ever and ever! Amen.*

Revelations 3:12 *Him who overcomes I will make a pillar in the temple of my God. Never again will he leave it. I will write on him the name of my God and the name of the city of my God, the new Jerusalem, which is coming down out of* *heaven from my God; and I will also write on him my new name.*

How can Jesus (pbuh) call himself "the Almighty" in 1:8 and also say that he has a God? It is a contradiction and nonsensical, just as many dreams are. Something else to ponder is if you believe Jesus (pbuh) to be God, then God is described in Revelations as an old man. This is something that gives atheists and agnostics reason to reject God.

Revelations 1:13 *and among the lamp stands was someone like a son of man, dressed in a robe reaching down to his feet and with a golden sash around his chest.*
Revelations 1:14 *His head and hair were white like wool, as white as snow, and his eyes were like blazing fire.*
Revelations 1:15 *His feet were like bronze glowing in a furnace, and his voice was like the sound of rushing waters.*

So Jesus in his essence is quite visible to John. Yet God is invisible and he can't be seen at anytime. If you see God you will die (Gen. 33:20). Perhaps this image of an elderly God, the continuous reference of Jesus (pbuh) to his God and the abstract details of the book of Revelations are what led Protestant founder Martin Luther to say that "Christ is neither taught nor known in it." (Luther's Works, Vol. 35, page 399)

IS JESUS (PBUH) SINLESS?

1Peter 2:21-22 *"...because Christ also suffered for us, leaving us an example, that ye should follow his steps: Who did no sin, neither was guile found in his mouth."*

Christians insist that Jesus (pbuh) was tempted by evil but he never succumb to evil and he remained sinless throughout his life. Some view this as evidence that Jesus (pbuh) is God. In the four gospels there are instances recorded that attribute lies and hypocrisy to Jesus (pbuh), and disrespect of Jesus (pbuh) to his fellow brothers, his elders and his own mother. Because I believe Jesus (pbuh) to be an upright prophet of God, I eschew such stories. Luckily, I do not have to reproduce or expound on these instances to demonstrate that sinlessness is not an automatic exaltation to divinity. I can merely cite the Bible and its records of others deemed sinless and righteous before God, thus making them Gods or disqualifying sinlessness as an evidence for Jesus' (pbuh) divinity.

Matthew 23:35 *That upon you may come all the righteous blood shed upon the earth, from the blood of righteous Abel unto the blood of Zacharias son of Barachias, whom ye slew between the temple and the altar.*

Hebrews 11:4 *By faith Abel offered unto God a more excellent sacrifice than Cain, by which he obtained witness that he was righteous, God testifying of his gifts: and by it he being dead yet speaketh.*

Daniel 6:4 *Then the presidents and princes sought to find occasion against Daniel concerning the kingdom; but they could find none occasion nor fault; forasmuch as he [was] faithful, neither was there any error or fault found in him.*

Luke 1:6 *And they (Zachariah and Elizabeth) were both righteous before God, walking in all the commandments and ordinances of the Lord blameless.*

DID PEOPLE THINK THAT JESUS (PBUH) WAS GOD?

One should consider what the people around Jesus (pbuh) thought of him. Did Mary think she was holding God in her arms when Jesus (pbuh) was a baby? Did the disciples think they were sleeping, eating, and ministering with God? Did the scribes and Pharisees think that they went antagonizing God?

Did the Romans soldiers feel that they were actually mocking and spit upon the creator of the universe? Did the Jews and Romans believe that they had crucified God? Even after the supposed crucifixion, did Mary Magdalene think God was a gardener? Did the disciples believe God ate broiled fish and a honeycomb? I would answer that these people probably did not believe Jesus (pbuh) was God, but that he was a man of power which was given to him by God as he said.

Some Trinitarians suggest that the disciples were persecuted and killed because of their belief that Jesus (pbuh) was God. This is a misrepresentation of the facts as well as a misrepresentation of the disciple's beliefs about Jesus (pbuh). First, we must realize that the disciples were persecuted because they would not pay tribute to the Roman emperor. At that time, the emperor was worshipped as a God, and because of their beliefs, the disciples would not partake in such activities. But what were their beliefs?

In Mark 4:34, Jesus (pbuh) says that he taught by parables, but he explained EVERYTHING to his disciples. Everything would include his divinity. When Jesus (pbuh) asked the disciples directly, "who do you say that I am?," what would you expect that they said? It is Peter who gives Jesus (pbuh) the correct answer.

Mark 8:29 *"You are the Christ."*

Matthew 16:16 *"You are the Christ, the Son of the living God."*

Luke 9:20 *"The Christ of God."*

Because of Peter's understanding, Jesus (pbuh) blessed him and declared that the foundation of his church will be built on the mindset of Peter. And Jesus (pbuh) also warned the disciples to tell no one who he was. Since it has been proven, that Messiah or Christ does not mean God, it's clear that Jesus (pbuh) did not teach them that he was God, only God's appointed messenger and that God's primary message is to worship him only. And the gospels inform us that the multitudes took Jesus (pbuh) to be a Prophet of God, as well.

Matthew 21:46 *But when they sought to lay hands on him, they feared the multitude, because they took him for a prophet.*

John 7:40 *Many of the people therefore, when they heard this saying, said, Of a truth this is the Prophet.*

Luke 7:16 *And there came a fear on all: and they glorified God, saying, That a great prophet is risen up among us.*

John 9:17 *And he said, "He is a prophet."*

Luke 4:24 *And he said, Verily I say unto you, No prophet is accepted in his own country.*

Luke 13:33 *Nevertheless I must walk to day, and to morrow, and the [day] following: for it cannot be that a prophet perish out of Jerusalem.*

Mark 6:4 *But Jesus, said unto them, A prophet is not without honour, but in his own country, and among his own kin, and in his own house.*

John 8:40 *But now ye seek to kill me, a man that hath told you the truth, which I have heard of God:*

These verses are documentation of what those living in Jesus' (pbuh) time thought of him. They were able to interact and converse with Jesus (pbuh). They were able to see him and touch him. They were eyewitnesses to his miracles. And they concluded that Jesus (pbuh) was a prophet of God and Jesus (pbuh) confirmed their understanding. Does this change after his time on earth?

Both Paul and John claim to have seen and spoken to Jesus (pbuh) after this time on earth. Paul says he saw Jesus (pbuh) in a vision and Jesus (pbuh) commanded him to teach the world about his mission. John says he saw Jesus (pbuh) in a dream and the story is told throughout the Book of Revelations. However, in the gospels Jesus (pbuh) never mentioned returning to talk to Paul or John or anyone. His return would be for the disciples to enter into heaven (John 14:1-3).

Nonetheless, we are presented with a DREAM of John, and the VISION of Paul. Both of whom attribute blasphemous claims to Jesus (pbuh), in which he never mention in his natural life, but mysteriously he decides to reveal this to them in visions. Does it make sense to explain his divinity in a dream or from a vision?

There is a multitude of evidence which demonstrates that Jesus (pbuh) did not claim to be God. And if he is God, he never articulated this in his lifetime, so why do it in a dream? His disciples had great troubles in understanding him in person. It is likely that John and Paul had similar problems from their mystic encounters with Jesus (pbuh). If they didn't have difficulties understanding Jesus (pbuh) in this manner, why did Jesus (pbuh) bother to get 12 disciples in the first place? He could have just come to earth and gotten crucified, then explain his mission in the vision's, without the heartache of trying to explain to the disciples.

EQUAL WITH GOD, AND OF NO REPUTATION

Philippians 2:5 *Let this mind be in you, which was also in Christ Jesus:*
Philippians 2:6 *Who, being in the form of God, thought it not robbery to be equal with God:*
Philippians 2:7 *But made himself of no reputation, and took upon him the form of a servant, and was made in the likeness of men:*

Philippians 2:8 *And being found in fashion as a man, he humbled himself, and became obedient unto death, even the death of the cross.*
Philippians 2:9 *Wherefore God also hath highly exalted him, and given him a name which is above every name:*
Philippians 2:10 *That at the name of Jesus every knee should bow, of [things] in heaven, and [things] in earth, and [things] under the earth;*
Philippians 2:11 *And [that] every tongue should confess that Jesus Christ [is] Lord, to the glory of God the Father.*

When Paul speaks of Jesus (pbuh) being in the form of God, he is speaking of the "image of God" which we found to be those who are righteous as God is righteous. But Paul takes things a bit further when he purports to know what Jesus (pbuh) THINKS. He said Jesus (pbuh) didn't think there is any fault in being equal with God. Even if Paul is trying to articulate that an extremely righteous and sinless person can be equated to God, he has made a grave mistake.

Job 25:4 *How then can man be justified with God? or how can he be clean [that is] born of a woman?*

In Job, we find that no man born of a woman can be compared to God. The Book of Job goes on to say that man is a worm in comparison to God (Job 25:6). Thus the most righteous person's piety is like a drop of water in the ocean compared to the Being which is the source of all righteousness and piety for every human being. If Paul meant to say that Jesus (pbuh) literally thought that he was equal with God, then Paul has a huge problem. Unlike Paul, I will show what Jesus (pbuh) thought through Jesus' (pbuh) own documented words.

A man came to Jesus (pbuh) and said "Good Master, what shall I do that I may inherit eternal life?" And Jesus (pbuh) said unto him, Why callest thou me good? [there is] none good but one, [that is], God (Mark 10:17-18). Before Jesus (pbuh) answered the man's question about how he is to get to heaven, which is extremely important, Jesus (pbuh) must first correct an issue of even greater importance. In the Bible, Jesus (pbuh) is not the most humble person (Matt. 12:6, Matt. 12:42, Matt. 12:41, John 8:53-56, John 4:12-14), but he makes it a point to show that he should not even be called GOOD, because only God is Good.

As the late great Ahmed Deedat once said "Jesus (pbuh) refused to even be called good. How would he react when you called him God?" So it seems that Jesus' (pbuh) THOUGHTS on the matter is that he is not equal with God. I submit to you that as with the rich man, Jesus (pbuh) would not answer any of your questions or accept any of your praise until he clarified that you should not call him God, for none is God except God.

In the verses of Philippians, we see that Jesus (pbuh) takes the form of God and the form of man. It is Paul who makes Jesus (pbuh) out to be something in between God and man. Paul is saying that Jesus' (pbuh) original nature is the reflection of God. Again, Paul does not realize that every human being who has ever lived was made in the reflection and image of God (Gen.1:26). God made every person upright or righteous (Ecc. 7:29). So, Paul is exalting Jesus (pbuh) for an attribute present in every human being who has ever lived.

In 1Timothy 2:5, Paul says "For there is one God, and one mediator between God and men, the man Christ Jesus." When we put these words of Paul with his words in Philippians 2:5-11, we find that Paul is certainly not calling Jesus (pbuh) God in these verses. Perhaps Paul is asserting that Jesus (pbuh) thinks it is acceptable to be equal with God in terms of righteousness. So God exalted Jesus (pbuh) and every person will confess to God the Father that Jesus (pbuh) is Lord.

Now, let's concentrate on Philippians 2:7. It is the King James Version which says that

Philippians 2:7 *But made himself of no reputation, and took upon him the form of a servant*

The modern translations are far less ambiguous. They translate the verse as "Rather, he emptied himself, taking the form of a slave" or something to the effect. As you will notice, there is a huge difference in the reading and understanding of these two translations. The former can be read without pause by a Trinitarian or an anti-Trinitarian. The later translation is a detriment to Trinitarians because it says that whatever power or glory that Jesus (pbuh) had, he set it aside to become a man, thus a man, not God, dead for their sins. This also would contradict Colossians 2:9, which says "For in him dwelleth all the fullness of the Godhead bodily." And if Jesus (pbuh) took on a human form and became limited then Paul is saying that God changed. But God says, "Surely I, the LORD, do not change" (Malachi 3:6). Philippians 2:7 must be taken metaphorically, if we are to possibly understand why Paul acknowledges the distinction between Jesus (pbuh) and God as he does in the following excerpts.

1Timothy 5:21 *I charge [thee] before God, and the Lord Jesus Christ, and the elect angels,*

1Corinthians 8:6 *But to us [there is but] one God, the Father, of whom [are] all things, and we in him; and one Lord Jesus Christ]*

1Corinthians 3:23 *You are Christ's and Christ is God's*

Ephesians 4: 6 *one God and Father of all, who is over all and*
through all and in all.

1Corinthians 11:3 *But I would have you know, that the head of every man is Christ; and the head of the woman is the man; and the head of Christ is God.*

In these last verses, Paul makes the ranks of the church crystal clear. God is in charge over Jesus (pbuh). And Paul also shows that Jesus (pbuh) has a God. If the manner in which Paul spoke of Jesus (pbuh) in relation to God confuses you, do not fret. The philosophers of his day thought him to be a babbler and a polytheist (Acts 17:17-18), and I can understand how they came to that conclusion.

A SCRIBE ASKS JESUS (PBUH) A CRITICAL QUESTION

Mark 12:28 *And one of the scribes came, and having heard them reasoning together, and perceiving that he (Jesus) had answered them well, asked him, Which is the first commandment of all?*

First of all, I must note that scribes were people who were experts in the laws of the Torah. This should prompt the reader to ask, "Why did an expert of the law ask Jesus (pbuh) such an elementary question?" Before one even considers Jesus' (pbuh) answer, please consider the reason for the question. Even if the scribe did not know the answer, which would be as preposterous as a Muslim not knowing the Shahadah, he could have asked any Tom, Dick, or Harry. Why did he ask Jesus (pbuh) of all people, this question?

Now, if the doctrine of the Trinity is true, then Jesus (pbuh) never explained the oneness of God. But I would submit to you that as a prophet of God, this explanation is paramount to his message. The first question anyone will ask a prophet is "what is this God like who sent you." Moses (pbuh) was aware of this fact, so he asked God, "Who shall I say has sent me?" (Gen. 3:13) And most assuredly, any expert of the laws of God would want to know what a supposed man of God has to say about the nature of God. With that said, let us analyze Mark 12:28-32.

<u>Mark 12:28</u> *And one of the scribes came, and having heard them reasoning together, and perceiving that he had answered them well, asked him, Which is the first commandment of all?*

As you see this scribe has already listened to Jesus (pbuh) preaching and he perceived Jesus (pbuh) to be a good teacher. Now Jesus (pbuh) brought certain revisions to many of the laws of Moses (pbuh) and this kind of thing would intrigue an expert of the law (Matt. 5:21-6:8). At this junction Jesus was discussing Moses (pbut), the laws of Moses (pbuh) and resurrection. This scribe accepted Jesus' (pbuh) revisions and his reasoning behind the revision (he says that Jesus (pbuh) answered well), but he knows that there is one law that cannot be revised and that is the first law. So, the scribe was testing Jesus' (pbuh) authenticity as a prophet of God with this question. As an expert, the scribe definitely knew the first commandment already. This is like a math teacher asking Albert Einstein, what is 2 plus 2. The teacher knows the answer, but she wants to know if Einstein will agree with her answer.

Mark 12:29 *And Jesus answered him, The first of all the commandments [is], Hear, O Israel; The Lord our God is one lord:*
Mark 12:30 *And thou shalt love the Lord thy God with all thy heart, and with all thy soul, and with all thy mind, and with all thy strength: this [is] the first commandment.*

This is the critical moment. They are engaged in a discussion about the commandment which deals with the very nature of God. This commandment is believed by every Israelite since the time of Moses (pbuh). If ever Jesus (pbuh) had an opportunity to say that he is God, or that God is three persons, it was right at that moment. But on the contrary, Jesus (pbuh) confirms this man's understanding of "GOD IS ONE."

Mark 12:31 *And the second [is] like, [namely] this, Thou shalt love thy neighbour as thyself. There is none other commandment greater than these.*

Then Jesus (pbuh) goes on to give the second commandment.

Mark 12:32 *And the scribe said unto him, Well, Master, thou hast said the truth: for there is one God; and there is none other but he:*
Mark 12:33 *And to love him with all the heart, and with all the understanding, and with all the soul, and with all the strength, and to love [his] neighbour as himself, is more than all whole burnt offerings and sacrifices.*

As you can see, the scribe acknowledges Jesus' (pbuh) answer to the second commandment, but in the scribe's mind, Jesus (pbuh) has already passed the test. He has made no changes to the nature of God (pbuh), as he did with the other aspects of the law. And the scribe adds to Jesus' (pbuh) answer "THERE IS NONE BUT HE." The scribe seemed to be suspicious of Jesus (pbuh) claiming divinity or he was apprehensive about Jesus (pbuh) teaching a new message. So this is where Jesus (pbuh) says, "wait, I am one of the three persons of God, right?"

Mark 12:34 *And when Jesus saw that he answered discreetly, he said unto him, Thou art not far from the kingdom of God. And no man after that durst ask him [any question].*

Jesus (pbuh) does no such thing. In fact, Jesus (pbuh) confirmed that the scribe had understood his answer correctly. Jesus (pbuh) declaring that this scribe spoke with understanding and that he was on the path to heaven. This dialogue becomes crystal clear proof that the Trinity is false because this man knew absolutely NOTHING of the Trinity. We must admit that this man believed God to be one, without three different personalities, yet Jesus (pbuh) affirmed that this man and every person who has ever followed the laws understood God's nature correctly. For Jesus (pbuh) to be God and not mention this fact, whether in private or in a parable, to a man of the law who required this very information from him, is a crime as a prophet of God. If he is one in the Trinity, then he lied and deceived this scribe. And I do not thing Jesus (pbuh) lied. This verse affirms what I have stated all along, Jesus' (pbuh) words totally refute the Trinity.

SOME FORSEEABLE REBUTTALS TO MY CLAIMS

1.) Jesus (pbuh) didn't know that he was one in the Trinity, so he didn't tell the scribe.
ANSWER-This in itself is blasphemy, if you consider that Jesus (pbuh) is God and at any moment he does not know his own identity.

2.) Jesus (pbuh) feared that the Jews would stone him for declaring his divinity.
ANSWER-Jesus (pbuh) on several occasions avoided the charge of blasphemy and the capital punishment that it carries. If you recall the famous incidents in which Jesus (pbuh) says "I and my Father are one" and "I am," both these times Jesus escaped punishment. He even avoided being thrown off a cliff after the Jews were enraged by remarks he made about Elias (pbuh) (Luke 4:28-29). Why does he become too fearful to say the most important thing that he knows? Or why doesn't Jesus (pbuh) just answer this man privately or in parable to explain the Trinity, if he FEARS the repercussions. I capitalize fear, to emphasize that GOD ALMIGHTY has no FEARS. This only

demonstrates that Jesus (pbuh) is not God. And to lie or deceive someone about his identity as God is blasphemy, which is far worse in the sight of God than the threat of death.

3.) Jesus (pbuh) deemed that people were not ready for such a comprehensive doctrine as the Trinity.
ANSWER-If Jesus (pbuh) is God, it should be no problem for God to explain something to someone. He is God! Who can do a better job? Paul? Why would God leave such a daunting task up to a mere man, when he is much more capable.

But wait. Is Jesus (pbuh) capable of explaining himself so others will understand? Jesus (pbuh) on numerous occasions admonished his disciples for their lack of understanding. He even called one of them "satan" because of his lack of understanding. God's (Jesus') most intimate friends could understand very little of what he told them. One of them denied ever knowing him (Mark 14:67-71), one of them led him to a torturous, grueling death (Matt. 26:47-48), and the remaining eleven, not only fell asleep three different times as he begged God to save him from death (Mark 14:41), but they forsook him and fled when he was captured (Mark 14:50). Jesus (pbuh) whom many believe to be God, spent 3 years with men who left their jobs and families to follow him and in 3 years GOD ALMIGHTY (Jesus) could not convince a single one of his followers to help him in his most critical hour. To ascribe such a monumental failure to GOD ALMIGHTY is outrageous.

Jesus (pbuh) is not God and there is no Trinity. What I have explained with Mark 12 has been consistent in my explanation of Jesus' (pbuh) words. Jesus (pbuh) does not declare himself to be God, at all. The question from the scribe and Jesus' (pbuh) answer proves that Jesus (pbuh) never taught his own divinity or that he is THE GREATEST DECEIVERS IN HISTORY OF MANKIND. Take your pick, but bear in mind

John 18:20 *Jesus answered him, I spake openly to the world; I ever taught in the synagogue, and in the temple, whither the Jews always resort; and in secret have I said nothing."*

THE LEAST FANTASTIC EXPLANATION

Now we have uncovered the fact that the Bible is lacking, in terms of defining the Trinity. In the four biographies (gospels) of Jesus (pbuh), not one of them records Jesus (pbuh) saying "worship me" or "I am God" or "That there are 3 persons and 1 God."

Upon first hearing this claim, a Christian may be in disbelief. The divinity of Jesus (pbuh) is engrained into their minds to such an extent that it is unfathomable that this claim is not explicitly stated in the Bible. However, the fact remains that it is not explicitly stated. Every verse used to demonstrate his divinity is implicit and susceptible to a different understanding as to its meaning.

If Jesus (pbuh) is God Almighty, not a single author of this life ever says that he is God. Yet all four Gospels record that Jesus (pbuh) rode a donkey into Jerusalem (Matt. 21:7, Mark 11:7, Luke 19:35, John 12:14). The Holy Spirit deemed it most important to inspire each and every author of the gospels to record that Jesus (pbuh) used a form of travel shared with everyone of that time, but it was of much less consequence to articulate, in a clear manner, the divinity of Jesus Christ (pbuh) and the oneness of God.

If you use Jesus' (pbuh) words, you must either conclude that he was not God or you have to admit that you are a polytheist because Jesus (pbuh) must be a lesser god than the Father. Though I have shown that the quotes in the Bible, theories and explanations used by Trinitarians are not supportive of the Trinity, some may still insist that the Trinity is consistent with the Bible. So, we are faced with a dilemma. If the Bible has two sides to a story, which side do you pick?

Perhaps the least fantastic proclamation is the truth. The side of the story that does not force you to change the word "God" into "divine," the one that does not need cats, ants and couches to be explained, the one that does not contradict one doctrine with another doctrine that attempts to explain it, the one that does not force you to say "by persons, I mean personalities," the one that does not have God having sex to beget a child, the one that does not need interpolated verses to support it. If my explanations are true, then this fantastic doctrine of the Trinity does not have to be explained. But one must explain how this can creep into the hearts and minds of monotheists, but not into the pages of the Bible without interpolations and implausible and/or impossible explanation.

FOR THE AVERAGE CHRISTIAN

Acts 2:22 *"O you men of Israel, hear these words: Jesus of Nazareth, a MAN approved of God among you..."*

PART V - MORE PROOF THAT JESUS (PBUH) IS NOT GOD

This section is a response to the average Christian. The average Christian is not familiar with the intricacy of the Trinity. They may not be able to articulate the explanations, theories and analogies of the Trinity. In most cases, they are armed with a few select verses (of which I have been discussing) and their complete dedication to defending and propagating their faith. In my experience, it seems that the average Christian holds some reservations about the divinity of Jesus (pbuh), yet they will immediately pronounce that "Jesus is God." When confronted with passages that accent Jesus' (pbuh) humanity, their reply is "well, he is the son of God?" Then I am forced to explain that the son of a monkey is a monkey. The son of a horse is a horse. The son of a man is a man. So the son of God is God. The task of explaining someone's belief to them and then refuting it becomes almost impossible, because the Christian doubts that I have presented his religion accurately in the first place. As a result, they go to their minister. He puts them at ease and convinces them that I am totally incorrect. You can imagine the difficulty presenting itself with me trying to debate a minister who is not there and a person convinced that I have no idea what I am talking about, however reasonable I may sound. With this in mind, I wish to simply list and document verses describing aspects of Jesus' (pbuh) life which show that he is not God.

-Jesus (pbuh) was in his mother womb (Luke 2:21)
-Jesus (pbuh) was circumcised (Luke 2:21)
-Jesus (pbuh) was hungry (Mark 11:12)
-Jesus (pbuh) was thirsty (John 19:28)
-Jesus (pbuh) wept (Luke 19:41, John 11:35)
-Jesus' (pbuh) family thought him insane (Mark 3:21)
-Jesus (pbuh) was angered (Mark 3:5)

-Jesus (pbuh) felt fear of men (John 7:1)
-Jesus (pbuh) felt fear of death (Mark 14:36)
-Jesus (pbuh) escaped persecution (John 10:39)
-Jesus (pbuh) was a carpenter (Mark 6:3)
-Jesus (pbuh) could sin (Heb 4:15), It is impossible for God to lie (Heb. 6:18, Num. 23:19)
-Jesus (pbuh) increased in wisdom (Luke 2:52)
-Jesus (pbuh) learned from experience (Heb. 5:8)
-Angels ministered to Jesus (pbuh) (Matt. 4:11)
-Jesus (pbuh) prays to God (Mark 6:12)
-Jesus (pbuh) is confused as to whether his witness is true or false (John 8:14, 5:31)
-Jesus (pbuh) will sit on God's right hand (Mark 16:19)
-Angel strengthens Jesus (pbuh) (Luke 22:43)
-Jesus (pbuh) is the way to God (John 14:6)
-The Father is greater than Jesus (pbuh) (John14:28)
-Jesus (pbuh) doesn't know the Day of Judgment (Mark 13:32)
-Jesus' (pbuh) power is given to him (Matt 28:18)
-Jesus (pbuh) had NO authority to speak on his own, he said what he was told by God to say (John 12:49)
-Jesus (pbuh) says none is good but one that is God (Luke 18:19)
- When Jesus (pbuh) was walking through a crowd, he didn't know who touched him (Mark 5:30/ Luke 8:45)
-Jesus (pbuh) says a mustard seed is the smallest seed on earth (Mark 4:31). This is not true.
-Jesus (pbuh) can't allow people to sit on with him on the right side of the Father, only God can (Matt 20:23)
-Jesus (pbuh) was weary (John 4:6)
-Jesus (pbuh) was tempted by the devil for 40 days (Luke 4:2),
God cannot be tempted (James 1:13)
-Jesus (pbuh) traveled in secret (John 7:10)

-Jesus (pbuh) rode a donkey (John 12:14)
-Jesus' (pbuh) words are from the Father (John 8:26)
-Jesus (pbuh) only speak what he was taught by the Father (John 8:28)
-Jesus' (pbuh) will is to please the Father (John 8:29)
-Jesus (pbuh) was captured (John 18:12)
-Jesus (pbuh) was put on trial (John 18:28)
-Jesus (pbuh) was ridiculed and beaten (John 19:1-3).
-Jesus (pbuh) was spat on (Matt. 26:67)
-Jesus (pbuh) was killed (John 19:30)

Just for a moment, consider that Jesus (pbuh) was God. Just substitute God for Jesus (pbuh) in this list and you will see the absurdity of such a claim. God was born with afterbirth, God suckle from a woman's breast, God soiled his diaper, God went to school and learned, God got in trouble with his mother, God passed gas and belched, God for 30 years of his life did absolutely nothing to help the world [aside from talking to some learned men as a 12 year old (Luke 2:42-47)]. What was he doing? Finally, God opens his mouth at the age of 30. And God is immediately attacked and God is scared and runs away. God never says "I am God," but he says "I am the son of God, BUT DON'T TELL ANYBODY." God was tempted by the devil to rule over EVERYTHING THAT IS ALREADY HIS. I can go on and on. God is a carpenter (I have often seen stickers which say "My boss is a carpenter, I wonder if it read "my God is a carpenter" would they feel any different), God rides donkeys and ultimately God is whipped, spit on and killed. As a child, I was told that God is almighty. No one can harm God and I am positive we all were taught this. However, it seems the story has changed. Now God can be afraid, beaten and killed.

Jesus (pbuh) is said to have been on the cross for approximately three hours and was taken off the cross dead. Most people survived on the cross for days. Crucifixion was meant to be a grueling, humiliating death that lasted for days. The fact that this crucifixion is not supposed to be completed in three hours is personified by Pontius Pilate's astonishment by the news of Jesus' (pbuh) death (Mark 15:44), along with the fact that the two criminals taken off the cross with Jesus (pbuh) were still ALIVE. How is it that God Almighty is not able to withstand the crucifixion as long as the average man? And is it not possible for God to forgive our sins without him being humiliated on a cross? If there exists a God in which the forgiveness of sin is possible without his torture, would you prefer the vulnerable or invulnerable God? I prefer the God that cannot be harmed EVER. THAT IS THE FATHER!

If you believe Jesus (pbuh) is God, then he is a God less powerful than the Father ("the Father is greater than I"), Jesus (pbuh) is not all knowing ("not that day knoweth not the son") like the Father, all his power is given to him ("I of my own self can do NOTHING") by the Father, and he has a God he calls on when he is in trouble ("my God, my God why have you forsaken me?"), who is the Father.

THE FATHER IS GOD

As I studied Islam as a teenager, I read that Prophet Muhammad (pbuh) was surrounded by idols and idol worshippers, yet he did not fall victim to worshipping their idols. I found this hard to believe. I read about the Prophet Abraham (pbuh) considering the worship of things other than ALLAH, and he rationalized his way to the belief in the one true God. I thought perhaps Muhammad (pbuh) did the same, yet it was not recorded. But one day I was compelled to think back to my childhood, in which several Sundays were spent in church. And I recalled that I never, ever believe Jesus (pbuh) was God, though I always believed in God. I can vividly recall sitting on the curb discussing the divinity of Jesus (pbuh) with my friend, who is ironically named Christiaan. We were both bewildered by the assertion that Jesus (pbuh) is God whom numerous people laid eyes on, yet it is purported that no one has seen God. This memory helped me to understand that it is possible to dwell in the heart of those with a particular belief and never accept this belief. As Prophet Muhammad (pbuh) did, you can stay true to the unseen God Almighty in the midst of those who deviate from the straight path. This is true amongst many Christians, I am sure. So, in essence, I always believed in the God the Father and never God the Son.

Jesus (pbuh) said no one has seen the Father or heard his voice (John 5:37). Therefore he is not the Father. The Father is the only being described in the Bible which bears all the attributes of God at all times. The Son and the Holy Spirit both originate from the Father. Jesus (pbuh) is begotten by the Father or he proceeded from the Father and the Holy Spirit proceeded from the Father, as well. In order for them to come from the Father, he must have been there first. There is no mention of the Father's origin, because he has always existed.

-Jesus (pbuh) instructs his followers to pray to the Father (Matt. 6:9).
-Jesus (pbuh) says the Father knows what the son does not know (Matt 24:36)

-Jesus (pbuh) says the Father is greater than him (John 14:28)
-Jesus (pbuh) says the Father is greater than ALL (John 10:29)
-The Father's will is superior to Jesus' (pbuh) will (John 5:30)
-The Father has the power which he distributes to Jesus (pbuh) (Matt 28:18)
-The Father is specifically called God by Jesus (pbuh) (John 20:17)
-In Jesus' (pbuh) time of need he calls the Father (Matt. 26:39)
-The Father is the God of Jews (John 8:54)
-The Father is perfect (Matt. 5:48)
-The Father rewards you (Matt. 6:1)
-Do the will of Father, you go to heaven (Matt. 7:21)
-Jesus (pbuh) thanks the Father, Lord of heaven and earth (Matt. 11:25)

From these verses it is abundantly clear that the Father is God Almighty. He is God in his totality, thus anyone added to him is belief in more than one God. Though you may read creeds and other doctrines using the phrases "God the Son" and "God the Holy Spirit," these phrases never appear in the Bible. "God the Father" is the only title which appears in the Bible (1Cor. 8:6, 1Thess. 1:1, Jam. 1:27, Gal. 1:1, 1:3, Eph. 6:23, Phil. 2:11, Jude 1:1, 2Tim. 1:2, Tit. 1:4, 1Pet. 1:2, 2Pet. 1:17, 2John 1:3). The fact that God and Father are used synonymously is documented throughout the New Testament (John 13:3, Eph. 1:2, 4:6, Phil. 4:20, Col. 1:2, 1Thess. 1:3, 2Thess. 1:1-2, 2:16, 1 Tim. 1:2, Philemon 1:3, 1 Pet. 1:3). And Jesus (pbuh) says of the Father that he is a spirit and he is God.

John 4:23 *But the hour cometh, and now is, when the true worshippers shall worship the Father in spirit and in truth: for the Father seeketh such to worship him.*
John 4:24 *God is a Spirit: and they that worship him must worship him in spirit and in truth.*

So everyone who believes in the Trinity must explain how the Father is the totality of God, all by himself. They must also explain how one of the godheads (Jesus) declares that the other (the father) is HIS GOD in his physical life as well as his spiritual life.

JESUS (PBUH) THE SERVANT OF GOD, NOT SON OF GOD

One theme that was been constantly repeated in this book is that Jesus (pbuh) is God's agent and messenger, not God himself. In Matthew 12:17-18, this sentiment is expressed clearly and it even comes with a reference to check its validity.

Matthew 12:17 *That it might be fulfilled which was spoken by Esaias the prophet, saying,*
Matthew 12:18 *Behold my servant, whom I have chosen*

Matthew is quoting Isaiah 42:1. The problem is that in Isaiah 42:5 the speaker is identified as God Yahweh or Jehovah. In Isaiah 45:5, this same Jehovah vehemently denies any partnership with anyone.

Isaiah 45:5 *I am the LORD, and there is no other; Besides Me there is no God.*

This is the totality of God claiming that he chose Jesus (pbuh) as his servant, thus excluding Jesus (pbuh) from the godhead. And if Yahweh or Jehovah is the Father, then again only the Father is God.

Translators of the Bible often times deceive the reader when it comes to translating the Greek word for servant, "pida." "Pida" means son, child or servant. In Acts 4:27, Jesus (pbuh) is called the holy son in many translations, including the most popular KJV. But two verses before this, David is described using the exact same "pida" and it is translated "servant." Honest translators recognized the obvious bias and interjection of personal belief into scriptures done by the other translators and now Acts reads as follows:

Acts 4:27 *"For of a truth against thy holy servant Jesus*

Acts 3:13 *"The God of Abraham, and of Isaac,..... hath glorified his servant Jesus."*

Acts 3:26 *Unto you first God, having raised up his servant Jesus*

When Jesus (pbuh) says the servant is not greater than the master (John 13:16), along with verses like 1Peter 2:18, it is clear that the master is greater than the servant. This is why it is so important to change the "servant" into "son." However both have implications of inferiority to the "master" or "the Father."

CONCLUSION

Do we really understand God becoming a man? To say God became a man is like saying a circle became a square. If a circle becomes a square, the circle is no longer a circle, but it is a square. In like manner, for the unseen, all powerful supreme immortal being to become a mortal corruptible, visible, vulnerable limited man, means he is no longer what he once was.

We are taught as children that God is the creator of all things. He is great, he is powerful, he is self-sustaining, he doesn't sleep or even feel fatigue, he needs nothing, nothing can harm him in the least, he knows everything, he is unseen, and he is without beginning or ending. No person who believes in God would refute a single one of these assertions. You may be hard pressed to find an atheist or agnostic to argue with you on these points. They are most antagonizing about the personalities and prerogatives given to the Supreme Being, not his nature if he does exist. When an atheist presents the theory of evolution and its claim that man and monkeys have the same ancestor, some people become incensed. They feel that this is unfathomable and unworthy of even being entertained. Yet these same people have absolutely no problem with God devolving into a human being.

This should be far more distasteful in their eyes. When a Hindu venerates an animal or a Buddhist sends prayers to Buddha, a Christian finds it odd. Yet they venerate and send prayers to God's creation (Jesus) and they find no fault in it.

Matthew 7:3 *Why do you notice the splinter in your brother's eye, but do not perceive the wooden beam in your own eye?*

Most of the 6.8 billion people of the world compromise and in some cases completely contradict the fundamental views of God's nature. Yes, there are more people on the earth who believe God was a man or animal, than those who believe in the unseen powerful God. Amongst the major religions of today, Islam and Judaism have a conception of a God who is powerful at all times and is never in need of anything or anyone at anytime. Yet the Jewish book of authority, the Jewish Torah (the first five books of the Old Testament), has some disparaging stories about God.

-God needs rest and to be refreshed (Ex. 31:17)
-God makes mistakes and regrets them (Gen 6:6)
-God cannot move iron (Judges 1:19)
-God can't see behind trees (Gen. 3:9)
-God is paranoid (Gen. 3:22-24)
-God hides his actions (Gen. 18:17)
-God gets advice from Abraham (pbuh) (Gen 18:22-33)
-God gets angry, Moses (pbuh) calms God down and God admits his error (Ex. 32:11-14)

Since the Old Testament paints God in a state less than Almighty, then this leaves Islam as the sole defender of the honor of God. This entire book up to this point has basically documented and explained the problem of man's understanding of God and his nature. I intentionally discussed the problem, with little reference to Islam, which has the solution to this problem. It was important to demonstrate that the Trinity can be dissected without using the Qur'an, but by using the Bible.

In anticipation for some backlash, I take full responsibility for any mistakes that I may have made. This is an extremely important topic to me. I would never attempt to deceive any person in the least. I am completely convinced that Jesus Christ (pbuh) and the Holy Spirit are no more than servants for the Father, who is the real God. I am so convinced that I would debate in public on this very topic.

All the evidence that I have surmounted is more than sufficient in my view for me to die and face my creator, if he were Jesus (pbuh) and say to him "I can prove to you from the Bible (or the Quran), that you are not God." The idea that one should just know and feel that Jesus (pbuh) is God can not be a means of my conversion. The faculty with which we comprehend is our mind. My brain cannot believe that Jesus (pbuh) is God amidst overwhelming evidence that he is not, no matter how many people confess to me their heartfelt belief that he is God.

There are millions of people who would have me believe that a cow is divine. Simply because one prayed to the cow and their life was changed, am I to abandon all my reasoning and logic and proof to the contrary and believe as they do? Not at all. The reason that blasphemy is such a severe sin is because it breeds disbelief or mistaken belief. If you think about it the story of Jesus (pbuh) as God is utter blasphemy. And all false religions are based upon some form of blasphemy. But man's blasphemy does not affect God. It affects man.

PART VI

AL-QURAN

I must first start out be saying that every aspect of the Trinity, of God and his nature, of the Holy Spirit and of Jesus (pbuh) believed by Muslims is firmly cemented in the Bible. Though, there are additions and for that matter subtractions from these scriptures, the truth can still be seen in the Bible. But a Muslim uses another book to arrive at and understand the truths in the Bible. He uses the Qur'an.

The Qur'an describes itself as the completion and criterion by which previous scriptures are measured. Of course, Prophet Muhammad (pbuh) has been charged with plagiarizing stories from the Bible. This claim is first challenged by the fact that Muhammad (pbuh) and most people of that time were illiterate.

Just as Moses (pbuh) had a speech impediment, yet God made him to speak grandly and authoritatively to the Pharaoh of his time, so too was Muhammad (pbuh) made to speak against the most learned and devoted people of other faiths, in his proclamation of the truth. He boldly told the stories of prophets, whom the Jews and Christians held dear, and he said to the audience, "what I speak is a correction of what you believe in." The proclamation is not the miracle. His inability to read and write is not the miracle. The miracle is that he was telling the truth.

If Muhammad (pbuh) copied the gospels, but he concluded that Jesus was not God, then he was right. As I have proven throughout, Jesus (pbuh) is not God. It is the Qur'an which informed the Muslims that others may say that Jesus (pbuh) is God, but Jesus (pbuh) never claimed to be God. And upon his investigation of the Jesus' (pbuh) words in the Bible, the Muslim finds that this is true. Therefore, Muhammad's (pbuh) supposed copy corrects the original. How is this so? The fact that he spoke so boldly, yet he was illiterate merely adds to the potency of his message. There are numerous examples of these corrections in the Qur'an, but I must focus on the issue at hand. I will explain the Qur'anic stand on the Trinity and its members and document verses from the Bible which corroborates the Qur'an, even though the Qur'an is in complete disagreement with most Christian's doctrines and their understandings. Let us begin with the Holy Spirit of Islam.

THE HOLY SPIRIT

The Holy Spirit is an angel of God which carries out God's commands. In Islam, an angel is considered to be a spirit, yet contrary to the Christian idea, angels cannot disobey God. Their nature is only to obey God's command. Consequently, we do not find the phenomenon of fallen angels in Islam. What we do find is spiritual beings called jinns, which have free will as man does to obey or disobey God. Shaitan or satan is a jinn in Islam, not a fallen angel. However since angels are by nature obedient to God, they all are Holy spirits. Yet the Qur'an does use the title exclusively for one angel in particular in the Qur'an. The Angel Gabriel's (pbuh) name is used interchangeably with the title "Holy spirit" in the Qur'an. This is not to say that the other angels are not Holy Spirit, but ALLAH bestowed titles upon angels and prophets which fit others but differentiate the individuals in discussion. This titling will be discussed further with regards to the titles of Jesus (pbuh).

Al-Qur'an 2:97 *Say, "Anyone who opposes Gabriel should know that he has brought down this (Qur'an) into your heart, in accordance with GOD's will, confirming previous scriptures, and providing guidance and good news for the believers."*

Al-Qur'an 16:102 *Say, "The Holy Spirit has brought it (Qur'an) down from your Lord, truthfully, to assure those who believe, and to provide a beacon and good news for the submitters."*

Al-Qur'an 26:192 *This (Qur'an) is a revelation from the Lord of the universe.*
Al-Qur'an 26:193 *The Honest Spirit (Gabriel) came down with it.*

We see in these verses that Gabriel (pbuh) is called the holy and the honest spirit in the Qur'an. And as we will see in the case of Jesus (pbuh), God takes great effort to help the reader to understand that the Holy spirit is not God. In each instance, God is the authority by which this revelation is revealed and he gives the Holy spirit power of attorney, so to speak, to deliver his message. This point is further illustrated when this "Spirit" brings glad tidings to Mary about the birth of Jesus (pbuh). Mary is understandably apprehensive about the situation and the presence of the "Spirit," with its resemblance to a man. The spirit says to Mary,

Al-Qur'an 19:19 *Nay, I am only a messenger from thy Lord, (to announce) to thee the gift of a righteous son.*

There have been certain Christian missionaries and apologist who attempt to persuade their audience to believe that the Holy spirit in the Islam is like that of the Holy Spirit in Christianity. The more accurate statement is that the Holy Spirit is similar to the Holy Spirit of the Bible, perhaps with a few exceptions, but far from the idea held by most Christians. It is obvious that the Islamic depiction of the Holy Spirit is not God, but he is God's.

Another accusation, which needs to be addressed, is the claim that the Holy spirit is not an angel, because there are verses in the Qur'an which seem to differentiate the spirit from angels. For example:

Al-Qur'an 78:38 *The day will come when the Spirit and the angels will stand in a row. None will speak except those permitted by the Most Gracious, and they will utter only what is right.*

Al-Qur'an 97:4 *The angels and the Spirit descend therein, by their Lord's leave, to carry out every command.*

This is just an honest mistake. In the language of Arabic, with the mentioning of a group of items, it is not uncommon to specify one part of the group to express emphasis. Examples can be found elsewhere in the Qur'an. In Surah or Chapter 2:238 God talks about prayer and the middle prayer is emphasized, but this does not negate the importance of the other prayers. In Surah 55:68 God talks about fruits, dates and pomegranate to emphasize the last two kinds of fruits.

Al-Qur'an 55:68 *In them are fruits, date palms, and pomegranate.*

Therefore we can conclude that Islam and the Qur'an accentuate the duty of the Holy Spirit mentioned in the Bible and they provide its proper meaning. The Holy Spirit is an angel which gives glad tidings, revelation, inspiration and strength by God's command.

JESUS (PBUH) THE SERVANT OF ALLAH

<u>Al-Qur'an 3:55</u> Behold! Allah said: "O Jesus! I will take thee and raise thee to Myself and clear thee (of the falsehoods) of those who blaspheme

One goal mentioned in the Qur'an is to clear the name of Jesus (pbuh) of those who blaspheme. In the time of Jesus (pbuh), there were many people who perhaps intentionally misunderstood Jesus (pbuh), to such an extent that they sought to have him crucified. And with all due respect, there are those who today misunderstand the man, Jesus (pbuh). For this reason, God seeks to clarify the message and the messenger from these inaccuracies.

Jesus' (pbuh) name is mentioned in the Qur'an, 25 times, whereas Muhammad's (pbuh) name is mentioned only five times in the Qur'an. I have seen in print the argument that because of this wide gap in name mentioning, the Qur'an holds Jesus (pbuh) in a higher esteem than Muhammad (pbuh). This argument is prepping its reader to believe that Jesus (pbuh) is God, even in the Qur'an. These are the same individuals who insist that Muhammad (pbuh) is the author of the Qur'an, not God. Thus Muhammad (pbuh) put someone else's name in the book more than his own. One problem with this reasoning is that Mary the mother of Jesus (pbuh) is mentioned 34 times in the Qur'an.

This would give her prestige over both Jesus (pbuh) and the supposed author of the book. Also, the name Moses (pbuh) is mentioned 136 times in the Qur'an. The problem with this logic is obvious. By their line of reasoning Moses (pbuh) is the better candidate for divinity. If Muhammad (pbuh) was the author of the Qur'an, wouldn't he mention himself twice as much as the other prophets? Wouldn't he mention his own mother, wife or daughter more times than he would mention Mary? He probably would. But because he was given the words to say from God by the Holy spirit, he is made to say that "we are to make no distinction between the prophets" (2:136) and he is made to clear the name of the prophets and give their true message.

The Qur'an is a message and guidance from God to humanity, not a biography, thus the message is emphasized not the messenger. This method, used to minimize the focus on Muhammad (pbuh) and maximize his message, has successfully kept the amazing and extraordinary character of Prophet Muhammad (pbuh) far removed from the idea of divinity. Muhammad (pbuh), considered by many historians to be the greatest man to have ever lived, in every sense of greatness (as a religious leader, a revolutionary, a general, and a king who looked after the people's well being, without taking advantage of his positions), is universally accepted as the servant and messenger of ALLAH by Muslims. And one message Muhammad (pbuh) conveyed was about Jesus (pbuh).

Al-Qur'an 43:59 *He (Jesus) was no more than a servant: We granted Our favor to him, and We made him an example to the Children of Israel.*

Al-Qur'an 3:49 *"And (appoint Jesus) an apostle to the Children of Israel, (with this message): "'I have come to you, with a Sign from your Lord, in that I make for you out of clay, as it were, the figure of a bird, and breathe into it, and it becomes a bird by Allah's leave: And I heal those born blind, and the lepers, andI quicken the dead, by Allah's leave; and I declare to you what ye eat, and what ye store in your houses. Surely therein is a Sign for you if ye did believe;*
Al-Qur'an 3:50 *"'(I have come to you), to attest the Law which was before me. And to make lawful to you part of what was (Before) forbidden to you; I have come to you with a Sign from your Lord. So fear Allah, and obey me.*
Al-Qur'an 3:51 *"'It is Allah Who is my Lord and your Lord; then worship Him. This is a Way that is straight.'"*

The first thing to note is that in these two chapters we see that Jesus (pbuh) is "no more than" a servant and an apostle of God. Though the line may be blurred in some parts of the Bible, this understanding of Jesus (pbuh) is to be found there (Acts 3:13, 26). It is also apparent that Jesus (pbuh) is sent to the children of Israel (Matt. 15:24), as the Qur'an states. And we notice that every miracle performed by Jesus (pbuh) is accompanied by the words "by ALLAH's leave." This is to make clear to you who is actually responsible for the miracles. The Qur'an attests to the fact that Jesus (pbuh) affirmed the laws and that he made some revisions to them (Matthew chapters 5&6). If the children of Israel were to obey Jesus (pbuh), they would in effect be obeying ALLAH. Not because he is God, but because he is God's spokesman. We find this same sentiment used for Muhammad (pbuh).

Al-Qur'an 4:80 *Whoever obeys the Messenger, he indeed obeys Allah.*

This same understanding should be used when Jesus (pbuh) says "the Father and I are one" and "he who has seen me has seen the father."

In these verses we also notice that Jesus (pbuh) says ALLAH is "my Lord and your Lord" (John 20:17). And obedience to Jesus (pbuh) is the way to God for the children of Israel (Luke 9:23). This message is echoed later in the Qur'an, with an addition pertaining to the Holy Spirit strengthening Jesus (pbuh) and ALLAH protecting Jesus (pbuh) from the persecution of the children of Israel.

Al-Qur'an 5:110 *Then will Allah say: "O Jesus the son of Mary! Recount My favour to thee and to thy mother. Behold! I strengthened thee with the holy spirit, so that thou didst speak to the people in childhood and in maturity. Behold! I taught thee the Book and Wisdom, the Law and the Gospel and behold! thou makest out of clay, as it were, the figure of a bird, by My leave, and thou breathest into it and it becometh a bird by My leave, and thou healest those born blind, and the lepers, by My leave. And behold! thou bringest forth the dead by My leave. And behold! I did restrain the Children of Israel from (violence to) thee when thou didst show them the clear Signs, and the unbelievers among them said: 'This is nothing but evident magic.'*

There are some Christians who would have Muslims believe that Jesus (pbuh) is the giver of life, due to the miracle mentioned of the bird made from clay. But this is a vain attempt to deceive the reader into understanding the opposite of what is read. In both chapters, anyone can see that God is the giver of life, not Jesus (pbuh). Another quick note is that the Qur'an says that ALLAH saved Jesus (pbuh) from the death on the cross, similar to what was written in the Gospels on the death and resurrection of Jesus (pbuh). Muslims are convinced that God is never in need of salvation and therefore Jesus (pbuh) could not be God.

__Al-Qur'an 4:157__ That they said (in boast), "We killed Christ Jesus the son of Mary, the Apostle of Allah";- but they killed him not, nor crucified him, but so it was made to appear to them, and those who differ therein are full of doubts, with no (certain) knowledge, but only conjecture to follow, for of a surety they killed him not:
__Al-Qur'an 4:158__ Nay, Allah raised him up unto Himself; and Allah is Exalted in Power, Wise;
__Al-Qur'an 4:159__ And there is none of the People of the Book but must believe in him before his death; and on the Day of Judgment he will be a witness against them;

In these verses we find that the Islamic view is that Jesus (pbuh) was not killed on the cross, but it appeared this way to those viewing and his supposed resurrection was, in fact, God saving Jesus (pbuh) from death and raising Jesus (pbuh) to himself. The "People of the Book" mentioned here are Jews and Christians.

As Trinitarians often suggest that Muslims should consider the possibility that we will be judged by Jesus (pbuh) as God of the universe, I would suggest that they should consider that Jesus (pbuh) will be a witness against their claims. Does the possibility that he is not God cross their minds at all? As documented throughout this book, Jesus (pbuh) did not teach his own divinity nor did he teach the doctrine of the Trinity. The Qur'an mentions the TESTIMONY of Jesus (pbuh) on the DAY OF JUDGMENT, before those who presume him and his mother have attributes of divinity.

Al-Qur'an 5:116 *And behold! Allah will say: "O Jesus the son of Mary! Didst thou say unto men, worship me and my mother as gods in derogation of Allah.?" He will say: "Glory to Thee! never could I say what I had no right (to say). Had I said such a thing, thou wouldst indeed have known it. Thou knowest what is in my heart, Thou I know not what is in Thine. For Thou knowest in full all that is hidden.*
Al-Qur'an 5:117 *"Never said I to them aught except what Thou didst command me to say, to wit, 'worship Allah, my Lord and your Lord'; and I was a witness over them whilst I dwelt amongst them; when Thou didst take me up Thou wast the Watcher over them, and Thou art a witness to all things.*

It has been the tactic of several evangelists to suggest that the mother and the son." They make this pronouncement because of verses like the one shown above, which denounce the worship of Jesus (pbuh) and Mary. But there are several problems with this claim. First, the Qur'an does not define the components of Trinity. This is only their assumption that the Trinity is composed in this manner. And how can they criticize the Qur'an for not describing the Trinity, when the Bible does not define or describe it? As documented earlier, the Trinity is an evolved doctrine and the Holy spirit was the last part of the godhead to be fully established and both were established by people hundreds of years after the Bible was written and after the life of Jesus (pbuh).

Al-Qur'an 3:78 *There is among them a section who distort the Book with their tongues: (As they read) you would think it is a part of the Book, but it is no part of the Book; and* *they say, "That is from Allah," but it is not from Allah: It is they who tell a lie against Allah, and (well) they know it!*

The Qur'an denounces all forms of the Trinity including the worship of Jesus (pbuh) and Mary as God. It is well known that there are Christians today who pay homage and submit their prayers to the Virgin Mary. And there were Christians in Arabia in the time of Prophet Muhammad (pbuh), who worshipped Mary called Collyridians. This idea may seem outrageous, but if we are to believe that she nurtured God Almighty for nine months and raised him to adulthood, then the Collyridians' conclusion seems inevitable.

Also, the doctrine of the Trinity have undergone great changes throughout history, thus it is possible to change again. So how can the Trinitarian possible indict someone for misrepresenting the Trinity? The retraction of the "begotten" son of god is an excellent example of change in the doctrine. Therefore it is advantageous for the Qur'an not to define the Trinity as it may be altered AGAIN. Not to mention that the Qur'an also says don't worship two gods (16:51), as well as three. What do they suggest that this means? It is clear that the Qur'an is dismissing the idea of any number of gods, besides one.

And the Qur'an addresses the Trinity from several logical standpoints. If the godhead consists of a father and a son, it is reasonable and logical to complete the exemplary family with a mother. The family relationship is the strongest bond humans can have together. Christianity insists that God the Father and God the Son have a relationship of love which exists forever.

And Christianity is called a relationship with God through his love. What love is more potent than a mother's love for her child? It is from this common knowledge that ALLAH denounces the Trinity. In the criticism of the idea of Jesus (pbuh) being the son of God, the Qur'an magnifies the improbability of a father and son of God without a mother.

Al-Qur'an 6:101 *To Him is due the primal origin of the heavens and the earth: How can He have a son when He hath no consort? He created all things, and He hath full knowledge of all things.*
Al-Qur'an 6:102 *That is Allah, your Lord! there is no god but He, the Creator of all things: then worship ye Him: and He hath power to dispose of all affairs.*
Al-Qur'an 6:103 *No vision can grasp Him, but His grasp is over all vision: He is above all comprehension, yet is acquainted with all things.*
Al-Qur'an 6:104 *"Now have come to you, from your Lord, proofs (to open your eyes): if any will see, it will be for (the good of) his own soul; if any will be blind, it will be to his own (harm): I am not (here) to watch over your doings.*

In this verse, we also notice that God's nature is explained. And in the Qur'an, this nature is never contradicted. God's nature is unchanging. He is creator of all things, he knows all things, no one can or has seen him ever, and he is above our comprehension. These attributes immediately eliminate Jesus (pbuh), his mother and the Holy Spirit. The words "he is above all comprehension" suggests that whatever we can possibly imagine, that is not God. Neither our eyes nor our mind can grasp God, "yet he is acquainted will all thing." In Islam, man knows God through his revelations and his attributes which are given to us by prophets of God. God has no wife and he is not in need of a begotten son.

Al-Qur'an 2:116 They say: "Allah hath begotten a son":Glory be to Him.-Nay, to Him belongs all that is in the heavens and on earth: everything renders worship to Him.

Just as with the case of the Trinity, the Qur'an presents the case of those who believe Jesus (pbuh) to be the begotten son of God and he condemns this exact belief as well as any belief in someone begotten by God. The Qur'an condemns this belief as one of the highest orders of blasphemy (5:27). We find in Chapter 19 that ALLAH says that the skies, the ground and mountain would cry out, if they had feelings like man, when such blasphemy is uttered against ALLAH, that a human being is his equal.

Al-Qur'an 19:88 They say: "(Allah) Most Gracious has begotten a son!"
Al-Qur'an 19:89 Indeed ye have put forth a thing most monstrous!
Al-Qur'an 19:90 At it the skies are ready to burst, the earth to split asunder, and the mountains to fall down in utter ruin
Al-Qur'an 19:91 That they should invoke a son for (Allah) Most Gracious.
Al-Qur'an 19:92 For it is not consonant with the majesty of (Allah) Most Gracious that He should beget a son.
Al-Qur'an 19:93 Not one of the beings in the heavens and the earth but must come to (Allah) Most Gracious as a servant.
Al-Qur'an 19:94 He does take an account of them (all), and hath numbered them (all) exactly.
Al-Qur'an 19:95 And everyone of them will come to Him singly on the Day of Judgment.

ALLAH is drawing our attention to the severity of this blasphemous claim. This, in turn, has Muslims combating this notion most vehemently. The diligence of the Muslims on this topic has caused Christian scholars, evangelists and apologists to redefine the word "begotten," eschew it or remove it all together.

Muslims are taught that "begetting" is an act that is beneath God. He can accomplish his goals without degrading or compromising his majesty.

Al-Qur'an 19:35 *It is not befitting to (the majesty of) Allah that He should beget a son. Glory be to Him! when He determines a matter, He only says to it, "Be", and it is.*

This is the Islamic concept of God, as it pertains to his creations. God merely wills things into being. God expresses the sentiment of his will as his word. God created everything from his word. Christians misunderstand this "word." They believe the word to be Jesus (pbuh) and since everything is created by God's word, they concluded that Jesus (pbuh) created everything. The Muslim's viewpoint is that Jesus (pbuh) is "A" word of God, not THE word of God. The Qur'an attests to this fact.

Al-Qur'an 31:27 *And if all the trees on earth were pens and the ocean (were ink), with seven oceans behind it to add to its (supply), yet would not the words of Allah be exhausted (in the writing): for Allah is Exalted in Power, full of Wisdom.*

Everything in existence, besides ALLAH, is his word and that word is "be." That word "be" became the stars, the moon, the trees and the sea. God's word materialized. And in the case of Jesus (pbuh), the same is true. The angels came to Mary give the good news of a son.

Al-Qur'an 3:45 *Behold! the angels said: "O Mary! Allah giveth thee glad tidings of a Word from Him: his name will be Christ Jesus, the son of Mary, held in honour in this world and the Hereafter and of (the company of) those nearest to Allah;*
Al-Qur'an 3:46 *"He shall speak to the people in childhood and in maturity. And he shall be (of the company) of the righteous."*
Al-Qur'an 3:47 *She (Mary) said: "O my Lord! How shall I have a son when no man hath touched me?" He(the angel) said: "Even so: Allah createth what He willeth: When He hath decreed a plan, He but saith to it, 'Be,' and it is!*

The famous Ahmed Deedat asked a Christian minister, would this minister prefer to give this account of the birth of Jesus (pbuh) to his daughter or tell her that "the Holy Spirit came upon her and the power of the Most High overshadowed Mary"(Luke 1:35). And this Christian minister bowed his head in shame and admitted he would prefer to give his daughter the Qur'anic version of the inception of Jesus Christ (pbuh). Can we blame him? This idea that God effortlessly creates has been a part of our thinking since childhood. And the Qur'an confirms this belief.

Also, in these verses, we find that the Quran clarifies Jesus' (pbuh) position after his life on earth. The Bible on numerous right hand of God." This innocent phrase has brought about great confusion. Some Christians perceive this position as a sign of Jesus' (pbuh) divinity and atheist and agnostics have fun questioning the literal interpretation given by Christians. The Qur'an however comes to the Christians' aid in this matter, with the simple words "of (the company of) those nearest to ALLAH."

This phrase better explains the "right hand of God" but it may not convey the exclusivity for Jesus (pbuh) which Christian desire. The Qur'an also lists some who will be in this elite group. There is clearly no distinction made between Jesus and other prophets (pbut) of God, as those nearest to God are not being spoken of geographically, but those who are the most righteous people.

Al-Qur'an 6:84 *We gave him Isaac and Jacob: all (three) guided: and before him, We guided Noah, and among his progeny, David, Solomon, Job, Joseph, Moses, and Aaron: thus do We reward those who do good:*
Al-Qur'an 6:85 *And Zakariya and John, and Jesus and Elias: all in the ranks of the righteous:*
Al-Qur'an 6:86 *And Isma'il and Elisha, and Jonas, and Lot: and to all We gave favour above the nations*

Al-Qur'an 4:163 *We have sent thee inspiration, as We sent it to Noah and the Messengers after him: we sent inspiration to Abraham, Isma'il, Isaac, Jacob and the Tribes, to Jesus, Job, Jonah, Aaron, and Solomon, and to David We gave the Psalms.*

Jesus (pbuh) is also called "a spirit proceeding from Him" in the Qur'an (4:171). This fact has often been misused by overzealous missionary to give Jesus (pbuh) some grand position beyond others in the Qur'an. Of course, their motives are always to conclude that in some way the Qur'an is affirming that Jesus (pbuh) is God. The first problem is that the very next verse mentions that Jesus (pbuh) served and worshipped ALLAH. The second problem is that the Bible equates a spirit with a prophet of God.

1John 4:1 *Beloved, believe not every spirit, but try the spirits whether they are of God: because many false prophets are gone out into the world.*
1John 4:2 *Hereby know ye the Spirit of God: Every spirit that confesseth that Jesus Christ is come in the flesh is of God:*

We see that a true prophet is a true spirit and a false prophet is a false spirit. And we can test this spirit/prophet to see if he is of God. So the title "a spirit proceeding from Him" is equal to the title "a prophet proceeding from Him." [Notice that the true spirit will confess that Jesus Christ (pbuh) has come in the flesh is true. Prophet Muhammad (pbuh) passed this test.]

The third problem is that every single person that every lived, has the spirit (ruh) of ALLAH in them. This is what gives us life. This lump of atoms called our body would only be a lump of atoms without the spirit or soul inside. The reason that the birth of Jesus (pbuh) is expressed with such emphasis on its details is because his birth was extraordinary. And more importantly it was misunderstood to mean that he is divine or the "unique" son of God. Every aspect of his birth was the same as every other person, aside from the fact that he had no father. This miracle, like every other miracle, was to show the power and proof of God. When people misunderstand and give the credit to the rabbit, instead of the magician, the magician reminds the people of another trick that he performed.

Al-Qur'an 3:59 *The similitude of Jesus before Allah is as that of Adam; He created him from dust, then said to him: "Be." And he was.*

ALLAH makes things so simple for us to understand. Most Muslims know this verse like the back of their hand, because it is so potent, yet so easy to convey. If Jesus (pbuh) is God because he had no father, than Adam (pbuh) is a greater God. He had no mother or father. In fact, he had no womb to grow. His body came from the earth and God blew his spirit (ruh) into Adam (pbuh) (38:72). His only guide and teacher was God. To a much greater degree, the idea of the son of God should be attributed to Adam over Jesus (pbuh).

THE TRINITY AND GOD THE FATHER

Al-Qur'an 5:72 *They do blaspheme who say: "(Allah) is Christ the son of Mary." But said Christ: "O Children of Israel! worship Allah, my Lord and your Lord." Whoever joins other gods with Allah,- Allah will forbid him the garden, and the Fire will be his abode. There will for the wrong-doers be no one to help.*
Al-Qur'an 5:73 *They do blaspheme who say: Allah is one of three in a Trinity: for there is no god except One Allah. If they desist not from their word (of blasphemy), verily a grievous penalty will befall the blasphemers among them.*
Al-Qur'an 5:74 *Why turn they not to Allah, and seek His forgiveness? For Allah is Oft-forgiving, Most Merciful.*
Al-Qur'an 5:75 *Christ the son of Mary was no more than an apostle; many were the apostles that passed away before him. His mother was a woman of truth. They had both to eat their (daily) food. See how Allah doth make His signs clear*

to them; yet see in what ways they are deluded away from the truth!
Al-Qur'an 5:76 *Say: "Will ye worship, besides Allah, something which hath no power either to harm or benefit you? But Allah,-He it is that heareth and knoweth all things."*
Al-Qur'an 5:77 *Say: "O people of the Book! exceed not in your religion the bounds (of what is proper), trespassing beyond the truth, nor follow the vain desires of people who went wrong in times gone by,-who misled many, and strayed (themselves) from the even way.*

When reading the Qur'an, we find that Jesus (pbuh) is often accompanied by the words "son of Mary," but never the "son of God." This is no coincidence. In fact, there are at least 99 names for ALLAH in the Qur'an, yet none of them is "Father." This omission is intentionally done to avoid the pitfalls of blasphemy, which many have fallen victim to. The Qur'an's attitude towards calling Jesus (pbuh) God is like joining gods with THE God, ALLAH. As seen earlier, Jesus (pbuh) shares none of the divine attributes of ALLAH. He is given his power and ability from ALLAH. Therefore to call him God, you must partner this inferior, subservient God to the supreme God. This leads us to the Trinity and its meaning in the Qur'an.

The actual word "Trinity" is not in the Qur'an, but the concept is mentioned in the Qur'an. This fact again nullifies the claim that the Qur'an has a misunderstanding of the Trinity. The words used and interpreted Trinity is "thalithun thalath," which means "a third entity from three." Upon examination we have found, despite the Trinitarians efforts and explanations to prove otherwise, that two of the beings of the Trinity, the Holy Spirit and Jesus (pbuh) are inferior to the one being in the Trinity who is actually the totality of God, the Father. Yet he represents a third of the godhead. This is polytheism, thus ALLAH insists that he is one without partners. Then ALLAH draws our attention to the fact that Jesus (pbuh) is one amongst numerous prophets. In essence, it is warning the reader not to make a mistake and hold your heroes as gods. Your heroes have all dead. ALLAH does not die. And then this verse defends Mary as a woman of truth. In other words, her words were true. So did she declare that she was God, or that she was pregnant with God or that the son of God was inside of her stomach, or did someone invent this? The Qur'an asserts that a truthful person like Mary would never have said such blasphemy.

The Qur'an then says "They had both to eat their (daily) food." This verse seems quite out of place. Was this a mistake? What does eating food have to do with anything? Well, ALLAH is simply trying to get the reader to think. The idea of God becoming a human being can be told with such grandeur that it seems like an amazing story. But this story can never be fully examined and incorporated in a human's everyday life. If it does, the whole idea falls apart. With this simple line, the Qur'an makes the reader go into the life of God, if he were a human being. If he were a human being, he would be hungry and thirsty, as Jesus (pbuh) was. And he would have to quench his thirst and feed his hunger. This is the furthest extent any Trinitarian will take you. But what happens after that. The body (of God) takes the nutrients it need from the food and beverage and emits the remainder. But how? Since ALLAH deems it less than suitable to articulate this, but he leaves it to the reader to conclude, I shall do the same. In short, being a human "does not befit the majesty of ALLAH."

ALLAH, like the Father of the Bible, does not die. Nor does he thirst or feel hunger. ALLAH does not eat food because he has no need for anything. The angels did not eat because they are not mortal beings, but spiritual beings. As Jesus (pbuh) suggests, man's state after death will be immortalized like an angel (Luke 20:36), yet Jesus (pbuh) ate food after his supposed death (Luke 24:43). Something to ponder. All these things should come to mind and perhaps more, when we examine this simple statement, "They had both to eat their (daily) food." The Qur'anic verse continues with an insistence for reader to notice how clearly and simply ALLAH brings truth to you. In other words, look how easy it is to recognize that these two people are not God. And anyone who eats food is not God. "Yet see in what ways they (Trinitarians) are deluded away from the truth!"

The Qur'an describes God in a nutshell with four short verses, which are so potent that it refutes every possible misconception of God on earth, in my opinion.

Al-Qur'an 112:1 *Say: He is Allah, the One and Only;*
Al-Qur'an 112:2 *Allah, the Eternal, Absolute;*
Al-Qur'an 112:3 *He begetteth not, nor is He begotten;*
Al-Qur'an 112:4 *And there is none like unto Him.*

The Qur'an says a man is not God, an animal is not God, the celestial beings are not God, but God is God. So simple, yet so many people do not understand.

THE TRUTH HAS ARRIVED

Though some may consider the mere mention of the Qur'an and the Bible in the same sentence as contemptuous, let alone studying one (the Qur'an) to understand the other (the Bible). recommend the study of both scriptures without intentions to insult anyone, but in all sincerity, as a path towards the truth. One may find that the Qur'an is incorrect in its assertions and now you are better equipped to pronounce this truth to the Muslims. Knowledge is power. And with this power comes the responsibility to enlighten others. The very idea of truth, insists that any other alternative is false. A fact found anyway (including the Qur'an) pertaining to truth, will only strength the truth and your conviction. Any falsehood juxtaposed the truth, will be exposed.

Al-Qur'an 17:81 *And say: "Truth has (now) arrived, and Falsehood perished: for Falsehood is (by its nature) bound to perish."*

I believe the truth to be contained in the Qur'an. The Qur'an says that Jesus (pbuh) is a prophet of God, and the Holy Spirit is an angel of God, thus making the Father, God. If this is bore in mind while reading the Bible, the message becomes clear. The same is true for the story of Jesus' (pbuh) crucifixion. The Qur'an says he was not crucified but it was made to appear to them (those who sought to kill him) so. If we read the Biblical account, there is more than enough proof to support this claim.

The Qur'an says that the Gospels were given to Jesus (pbuh). If we open the New Testament, we find that the Gospel of Jesus (pbuh) is nowhere to be found. We find four biographies of Jesus (pbuh), which are the gospels of four unknown men. Though Muslims consider Jesus' (pbuh) message contained in these biographies to be incomplete and in some cases altered, the Muslim will say that if you follow the words of Jesus (pbuh) alone, you would be a Muslim. That is to say that those who pride themselves as being followers of Christ have been led off the tracks and the Muslim belief is synonymous to the teaching of Jesus (pbuh). How stupendous or outlandish, depending on your point of view, is this proclamation? This claim begs for investigation, to be proved or disproved. The religion of Islam is defamed everyday on television, in movies and in the media, yet it remains the fastest growing religion in America, in England and in the world with very little propagation. And in the face of this vilification, any Muslim will tell you that the Jesus (pbuh) described in the Bible is a Muslim. Perhaps, if Christians ventured into this claim, they would find themselves on the side of the Muslim.

Al-Qur'an 5:82 *...and nearest among them in love to the believers wilt thou find those who say, "We are Christians": because amongst these are men devoted to learning and men who have renounced the world, and they are not arrogant*

It is my intention to broadcast the truth of Islam to the world. There are those who spend every waking day in contention with Islam. Many of them are sincere, yet there are those who conjure up the most audacious lies known to man. These people thrive upon the fact that most people have not read the Qur'an and have no intentions of reading it, and that people confuse other countries' culture with Islam. The perception is that many Muslims at this time are either fanatics not willing to have a dialogue, they are oppressed and ill-equipped to have a meaningful dialogue or they are emasculated and afraid to have a dialogue. But every Muslim is commanded to

Al-Qur'an 16:125 *Invite (all) to the Way of thy Lord with wisdom and beautiful preaching; and argue with them in ways that are best and most gracious: for thy Lord knoweth best, who have strayed from His Path, and who receive guidance.*

There are websites and books listing the supposed contradictions and difficulties in the Qur'an, as well as half quoted verses of the Qur'an portraying Islam as a religion of war and forced conversions. I have participated in numerous debates and I have come to the conclusion that anyone who attempts to persuade another person that Islam is a religion of war and forced conversions, falls under two categories. They are sincere but not well versed in their accusations or they are blatantly deceitful. I say this because any verse used to promote these accusations must be used separate from its context. I would ask them simply to read the verses before and after the verses that they cited. In every instance, their folly or deceit becomes evident.

As it pertains to the allege contradictions and difficulties, I find that almost all of these claims originate from the internet. There is a website composed of mainly atheists and agnostics, which is visited by Christians and Jews to built their arsenal against Muslims. I found it rather peculiar that the Christians, Jews and Hindus, who visit this site, make no effort to convince their friends to believe in God, but it is of greater importance to pat each other on the back for finding a new tactic to combat Islam.

I visited this site and I was at first taken aback. But I later felt it a compliment for Islam to be considered such a formidable opponent that it warranted alliances of the God fearing as well as the godless. I challenged the validity of these claims against Islam. As a layman, amidst many who spoke Arabic, I felt that ALLAH helped me to get my points across, which including a dialogue about the existence of God. One can find the accusations against the Qur'an and Islam, just as a non-Jew or non-Christian might find accusations against the Bible. Just use the simple steps of placing the words "contradictions of the Qur'an" in your search on the computer. You will find a long list of things. I suggest first that you check them up yourself before repeating them to others, especially Muslims. Because he may use the simple steps that you followed and add the words "refutation of" (the contradictions of the Qur'an) and he will find the answer to every single question you raise against the Qur'an and Islam. This is because Islam and the Qur'an are the truth.

Al-Qur'an 32:2 *(This is) the Revelation of the Book (the Qur'an) in which there is no doubt,-from the Lord of the Worlds.*
Al-Qur'an 32:3 *Or do they say, "He has forged it"? Nay, it is the Truth from thy Lord, that thou mayest admonish a people to whom no warner has come before thee: in order that they may receive guidance.*

Made in the USA
Middletown, DE
05 January 2024